P

NICHOLAS KING

LONDON UNITED

LONDON CENTRAL

METROLINE

EAST LONDON

SOUTH LONDON

SELKENT

LEASIDE BUSES

CENTREWEST

LONDON GENERAL

LONDON NORTHERN

Capital Transport

Sixteenth edition 1993

ISBN 185414 156 2

Published by Capital Transport Publishing
38 Long Elmes, Harrow Weald, Middlesex

Printed by Winchmore Press
Fowler Road, Hainault, Ilford, Essex

The cover photographs are by Stephen Madden (front) and Russell Upcraft (back)
The photograph on page 4 is by R.J. Waterhouse

CONTENTS

Standard body codes are used throughout this publication, showing the body type, seating capacity and entrance position in that order.

Body Type	Single-deck bus	B
	Single-deck coach	C
	Double-deck coach	CH
	Dual-purpose vehicle	DP
	Highbridge double-deck bus	H
	Open-top double-deck bus	O
Seating capacity	For double deckers the upper-deck capacity is shown first, followed by that for the lower deck.	
Entrance Position	Separate entrance and exit (front and centre) with doors	D
	Front entrance with platform doors	F
	Rear entrance without doors	R
	Rear entrance with platform doors	RD
	Tail-lift fitted	L

INTRODUCTION

This book gives details of the bus and coach fleet operated by London Buses Ltd and its subsidiaries at 1st June 1993, when 56 classes totalling 5,246 vehicles were held. Another 136 vehicles were on order, bringing 2 further classes into the fleet.

New classes to have appeared since the last edition include the SP batch of Optare Spectra double-deckers and the GLS class of Leyland Nationals rebuilt to Greenway specification. On the debit side the OV class of Optare City Pacer minibuses has disapeared, as have classes unique to London Coaches, which have been transferred to *London Bus Handbook Part 2* following sale to a management-led team in May 1992. The DMS/D classes have been withdrawn from normal scheduled service (although a handful remain for special purposes including private hire work and training), and the LS class has been reduced to the Red Arrow fleet, 17 vehicles with Westlink, ten with CentreWest and six mobility buses. Withdrawal has started of the Leyland Titans. Forthcoming arrivals include further midibuses, full-size single-deckers, and 68 low-floor single-deckers.

The RML fleet is being refurbished to carry it into the next century, and most have been equipped with Cummins or Iveco engines. Only 86 standard RMs remain scheduled for service, though many others remain as engineering spares for RML allocations and to cover the refurbishment programme.

The London Forest subsidiary ceased trading in November 1991. During 1993/4 the programme to privatise the remaining subsidiaries is expected to gather pace. Meanwhile, moves towards greater efficiency are involving the closure of several garages. East London opened a midibus base at Stratford in September 1992, closed West Ham in October 1992 and shut down Seven Kings on 20th March 1993. CentreWest closed Hanwell on 27th March 1993, upgrading Acton to big bus status and opening a new midibus outstation at Greenford. Metroline reduced Edgware to an outstation on 6th March 1993, upgrading Cricklewood to full garage status instead. London Central are closing Peckham in June 1993, replacing it with an outstation at Copeland Road and moving most big buses to Camberwell and New Cross. London United have opened a new base at Wood Lane for midibuses previously working out of Shepherd's Bush. South London have mothballed their new garage at Streatham after just five years. London General are closing Victoria garage.

This book also includes details of the fleet of ancillary vehicles operated by London Underground Ltd for subsidiaries of London Transport. Most of these are leased, although a few heavier vehicles continue to be purchased outright. Details are also given of such vehicles owned directly by the operating subsidiaries.

The author gratefully acknowledges the willing assistance of staff of London Transport, and in particular the help given by Lawrie Bowles, Kenneth Fahy and Keith Smith. Thanks are also due to Colin Lloyd and David Stewart of the London Omnibus Traction Society, to Mark Jameson, and to the PSV Circle. Whilst this book is based on information supplied officially, it should be emphasised that it is not an official publication of London Transport, nor of London Buses Ltd. Any enquiries should be addressed to the publisher.

Readers requiring further information on developments within the fleet are recommended to consult the news-sheets of the enthusiast bodies mentioned above.

Hemel Hempstead, June 1993 — NICHOLAS KING

ROUTEMASTERS

Four prototypes of the Routemaster were built, RM 1 at Chiswick in 1954, RM 2 in 1955, RML 3 (later RM 3) by Weymann in 1956 and CRL 4 (later RMC 4), a Green Line coach, by Eastern Coach Works in 1957. RMC 4 passed to London Country Bus Services Ltd on 1st January 1970 and to London Country South West on 7th September 1986, remaining in use for special occasions. RM 3 was sold for preservation in February 1974 whilst RMs 1 and 2 were transferred to the London Transport Museum on 31st March 1985. The early development of the production batch is detailed in earlier editions of this Handbook.

In 1961 a trial batch of 24 Routemasters (RML 880-903) was built to 30ft length. An additional short bay was added to the body and these vehicles had a capacity of 72, being classified 7RM7. The type first entered service at Finchley garage on the then route 104 on 8th November 1961. Following trials conducted on RMs 632, 870 and 1009, some batches of RMs were equipped with Leyland units.

Perhaps the most interesting variant of the RM design was the front-entrance RM developed by AEC and Park Royal with a view to marketing the Routemaster outside London. Numbered RMF 1254, this vehicle never ran in service in London, being used for a short period as a demonstrator before passing to the BEA fleet and thence to Northern General Transport, who alone placed orders for a total of 50 Routemasters. RMF 1254 was purchased for preservation in 1981. Twelve of the Northern General vehicles were purchased by London Transport in 1979/80 but were sold in 1981 without ever being commissioned.

Sixty-eight Green Line Routemaster coaches were delivered in 1962 as RMC 1453-1520. They passed to London Country in January 1970, and most returned to London Transport between 1977 and 1979 for use in the training fleet. Two remain in stock for this purpose. In addition to the trainers, RMCs 1464, 1510/5 have been converted to open-top for use at Norwood, Westbourne Park and Upton Park respectively, and seven others were refurbished in 1989 and entered service in red and gold livery on Beckton Express route X15 from Upton Park garage on 6th March 1989. This route has since been converted to opo, and the RMCs make occasional appearances on the 15.

The last production standard RM built was RM 2217. Construction was then standardised on the 30ft version, starting with 43 Green Line coaches (RCL 2218-2260). These were followed by a further 500 standard RML buses, of which 100 were delivered in Country Area green livery. The RCLs and 97 of the green RMLs passed to London Country in January 1970; like the RMCs, most returned to London Transport at the end of the 1970s. The RMLs were then painted into red livery and entered normal passenger service. The RCLs were chiefly used as trainers, except for RCL 2221 which was converted as a cinema and exhibition bus. After serving in this role RCL 2221 remained as an exhibition vehicle and is still available for hire in this guise. The remaining RCLs were overhauled during 1980 and returned to passenger service without their platform doors. They were taken out of commission between 1983 and 1985 and most were sold, although eleven which remained in stock at the end of 1985 were adapted for use in the London Coaches fleet.

In October 1966 RML production was suspended to enable the construction of 65 front-entrance Routemaster coaches specially adapted for the needs of British European Airways transfer services from Heathrow. These buses were owned by BEA (later British Airways). Rationalisation of services and the abandonment of the check-in facility at Gloucester Road led to a reduction in the requirement for these vehicles and in 1975 thirteen surplus vehicles were sold to London Transport. They were repainted red and entered service on the 175 from 11th October 1975, but were withdrawn from this work within a year. After a period during which their future was assessed three were converted to driver trainers. A further 14 vehicles were purchased in November 1976, followed by the remaining 38 in June 1979. They were generally placed into use as staff buses, many still in British Airways colours, although another seven received modifications for use as trainers during 1981. The continuing reappraisal of requirements for staff buses and trainers during the 1980s resulted in most of the RMAs being sold, especially following the closure of LRT Bus Engineering Ltd, and just one remains in use as a trainer. Another two were refurbished as private hire vehicles and as spares for Beckton Express route X15; like the RMC buses, they still make occasional appearances on the 15 from Upton Park.

During the latter half of the 1960s work was in hand on the development of a front-entrance, rear-engined Routemaster. This appeared as FRM 1 during 1966. The project did not develop further and FRM 1 eventually found its way to the London Transport Museum on 17th May 1984.

A total of 199 RMs were fitted with illuminated offside advertisement panels following trials with RM 1577, and 100 of the red RMLs delivered in 1966/7 also had this feature. The RMs attracted the body coding RM9 whilst the RMLs were coded RM7/5. When Aldenham overhauls finished in 1985 these bodies were carried on RMs 796, 1528, 1849, 1906/16/24-6/9-34/6/9-47/9-56/8-67/9-2004/6-19/21-2127, many of which have now been sold, and on RMLs 2527/44/61-7/9-76/81-2647/9-60/2/4, 2759. In most cases these displays have now been covered with conventional vinyl advertisements, and some have had the illuminated panels covered over or replaced by standard flat panelling. However, two which had been so modified have since reverted to original condition at Tottenham.

RM 5, notionally the first production RM, has been retained as a showbus and currently operates from Clapton on the 38. A few other RMs and RMLs are kept in showbus condition.

RML 890 was equipped with Capital Radio in the upper saloon in October 1986 and is currently in use at Upton Park on the 15.

RML 903 was repainted and prepared for a number of special events including an extended trip to Scotland and a goodwill visit to Holland in September 1987. It has continued to operate on route 13 from Finchley garage in this condition.

For several years a significant proportion of the standard RM fleet was required for training duties, though this usage has declined following the introduction of revised legislation in April 1991. A small number of RMLs are also designated for type-training and appear on normal service when not so required.

In September 1982 some 200 RMs became redundant, and withdrawal of the class has continued remorselessly since then. The RML fleet has however remain intact, apart from isolated casualties, and has gradually moved onto the busier routes serving the West End. As part of this process several established routes were converted to opo at their outer ends, leaving the heavily-trafficked central section in the hands of RMLs, and the conversion of all Sunday Routemaster routes to opo was completed in August 1990. An increasing number of Routemaster routes are now succumbing to opo on weekday evenings, and few thoroughfares are now exclusively the domain of Routemasters during the daytime, the most significant probably being Piccadilly, the entire length of which is still Routemaster territory.

Fifty RMs were transferred to the newly-formed London Coaches fleet in January 1986, many of these becoming open-toppers. Another interesting variant of the RM appeared in January 1990 when ten of the open-toppers were taken to Kent Engineering (Canterbury) and rebuilt with an extra full-length bay, increasing the capacity to 76. These formed the ERM class, now held by the privatised London Coaches fleet. Only as a result of the jig-built modular construction of the Routemaster could such a project have been feasible. Proposals to carry out a similar lengthening of a covered-top Routemaster were not, however, developed.

Because of the increasingly-limited future security of AEC engines, RM 1894 was fitted with an Iveco engine during 1988, and RM 545 received a DAF engine. RM 2033 followed with a Cummins engine in mid-1989, and RM 1128 received an

Ashok engine (after the abandonment of plans to fit Volvo units). RM 825 was to have received a Pezetel engine, but this did not occur. Following the conclusion of these trials, the majority of surviving Routemasters were fitted with Cummins or Iveco engines, a final batch of 98 RMLs receiving Cummins units at the turn of 1992/3. A number of standard RMs fitted with Iveco units in the earlier stages of the programme were withdrawn during 1992 and their engines transferred to RMLs as part of the conversion programme. A small number of Routemasters still carry AEC units, but the last Leyland-engined example was delicensed in April 1993.

Major refurbishment of the RML class to carry the type into the next century is now in hand. In the summer of 1991, RMLs 2648 and 2735 were extensively rebuilt, both mechanically and structurally. These and RML 2313 re-entered service in July 1991 with three different interior designs, followed by RML 2715 in the autumn of 1991. At the same time, RM 994 was given a mini-refurbishment by Northern Counties, although this is to remain unique. The main programme involving 486 RMLs (subsequently increased to 490) started in January 1992 and is planned for completion in 1994, with 46 vehicles being prepared by Leaside Buses and painted at Hants & Dorset Engineering, and the others being divided equally between T.B. Precision of Birmingham and South Yorkshire Transport. The final specification includes new upholstery and interior trim, concealed fluorescent lighting in both saloons, new flooring and complete body overhaul, whilst mechanical items include complete replacement of braking and electrical systems and of the B-frame. Twenty-four refurbished RMLs were leased via London Transport to Kentish Bus in April 1993 in conjunction with the LT tendering of route 19, and now carry Kentish Bus livery.

Victoria garage has fitted platform doors from a withdrawn RMC trainer to RML 2516. Unofficially carrying fleet number DRM 2516, this vehicle is intended for use on private hire work and the London By Night sightseeing tour, working alongside normal Routemasters (with rear doors normally open) at other times.

In April 1989, RM 89 and RM 1590 were repainted into London General livery to mark the launch of that new subsidiary. These are currently allocated to Putney and Victoria garages respectively. RML 880, at Shepherd's Bush, followed in traditional-type London United livery in May 1989 and carries fleet number ER 880, with which it was originally delivered.

Many Routemasters have surrendered their original registrations to other vehicles since 1987, receiving A- or B-suffix registrations instead. Since February 1992, non-transferable unsuffixed registrations have been issued to pre-1963 vehicles in such cases. Many remain in service with their new registrations.

The standard RM class is now officially restricted to six garages: Brixton (for 159), Chalk Farm (for 139), Victoria (for 11), Holloway (for part of 10), Peckham (for 36) and Camberwell (for 159). However, many others are in use to cover the RML refurbishment programme and to act as engineering spares to RMLs. As described above, two RMAs and seven RMCs occasionally appear on the 15 from Upton Park, and three RMCs survive in open-top form. RM 644 is a further open-topper, transferred from London Coaches to Metroline at the start of 1992.

DMS/DM/D

In 1965, London Transport took delivery of eight Daimler Fleetlines for experimental trials alongside 50 Leyland Atlanteans and, from 1967, the FRM. The eight Fleetlines, in Country Area green livery, passed to London Country on 1st January 1970. As a result of these trials, however, 17 Fleetlines with Park Royal bodywork were ordered for Central Area use from 1969, followed by another 100 for 1970. The combined order entered service from January 1991 as the DMS class, and a further 1,850 vehicles were ordered for the period up to 1974, bodied by Park Royal and Metro-Cammell-Weymann. Of these, 460 were delivered with modifications to suit them for crew operation and were classified DM; when later transferred to opo work, they were recoded D.

DMS 854 was delivered with experimental quiet features and became the testbed for the Leyland B20 project. Orders for 1975/6, now under the Leyland marque, specified another 279 standard Fleetlines and 400 B20 types. The last Fleetline was delivered on 23rd August 1978.

The B20 vehicles had substantial external design differences, most notably at the rear, where the engine shrouds were replaced by two chimneys with angled air inlet and exhaust grilles projecting upwards from the engine compartment on either side of the rear window.

Withdrawal of the Fleetlines commenced in 1978 when a substantial number of long-defective vehicles were sold for scrap following a decision that the type was not best suited to London's needs. Most of the non-B20 vehicles had been taken out of passenger service by 1983. DM class vehicles were gradually converted to D type for opo use from 1979, although this process was not completed until early in 1987. As service requirements diminished, several Fleetlines were transferred to training duties. DMs 948 and 1102 were converted to open-top and remain in use with Selkent for special duties. DMS 2291 was converted to open-top during the spring of 1988 following a lowbridge accident, and D 2556 followed for Holloway in October 1992.

By the end of 1985 the majority of Fleetlines surviving in service were concentrated in the then-Wandle District and were of the B20 type. A major programme was undertaken to refurbish and repaint them, and 100 were fitted with Iveco engines in 1987/8, followed by a further 101 during the spring of 1989. They were gradually replaced during 1991 and 1992, DMS 2438 being the last in normal service at Croydon at the end of January 1993. A handful of Fleetlines remain placed for private hire and other special duties at Stamford Hill and Holloway, others serve as training vehicles. Of these, most of the London General trainers have received yellow fronts and unofficial DMT class codes. DMS 1657, in Bexleybus livery, is on extended hire to the Metropolitan Police Training College at Hendon for demonstration purposes in training police recruits.

M

London Transport ordered a trial batch of five MCW Metrobuses in 1977 following the operation of 164 Scania Metropolitans (MD class) from 1975. The first Metrobus was delivered on 21st April 1978, and all of the first five carried blind boxes of DMS style, although subsequent arrivals had displays in which the route number and via point blinds were combined. A total of 200 Metrobuses were ordered for 1978/1979 delivery, followed by a further 300 up to 1980.

The 1981/2 order of vehicles called for an additional 300 which embraced an updated mechanical specification, although remaining outwardly almost identical to the earlier deliveries. M 606 upwards were delivered with red-painted grilles, and M 706-805 had a revised grille design. Because of this specification change these vehicles were at first concentrated in Leaside District, except for six which were experimentally sent to Sidcup for comparative trials alongside Titans, remaining there after the end of the trials until its closure in May 1986.

Further batches of 150 vehicles for each of 1983 and 1984 and another 335 for 1985 completed the main sequence of Metrobus orders. By this stage the need to segregate vehicles with minor differences of equipment had been abandoned and all basic Metrobuses up to 1440 are now allocated freely as required.

Ms 1006-1029 form the current Airbus fleet and have coach seating, carpets upstairs, and substantial luggage lockers in the lower saloon. These entered service from 14th April 1984 at Stamford Brook garage. During 1987 they were fitted with Ratcliffe lifts in the central doorway to enhance their accessibility by the disabled, together with anchor-points for two wheelchairs in the lower saloon. All of these vehicles were fully-refurbished in 1992, losing two upper-deck seats in the process. More recently, Ms 19, 39, 43, 86, 96 and 162 have been modified as standby vehicles for summer loadings, though not receiving tail-lifts or other refinements.

M 1084-1105 are fitted with Cummins engines. These entered service at Brixton garage from 19th November 1984. They are all now based at Croydon

The specification for all 1440 Mk1 Metrobuses includes the fitting of Gardner 6LXB engines (except for the 22 Cummins vehicles) coupled to a Voith gearbox incorporating torque converter and retarder.

A Deutz air-cooled engine was fitted to M 205 at Chiswick during 1985 and this vehicle entered service at Brixton in the autumn of 1986 after extensive trials. The Deutz unit was replaced by a standard Gardner unit in the spring of 1990.

M 919 visited Ogle Designs at Letchworth for assessment in connection with cab modifications in November 1983. M 817 has been fitted with a modified driver's seat, and from M 956 onwards the driver is able to change all front blinds from the cab, rather than just the ultimate display, and different cab windows are also fitted. From M 1279 a further revised front grille has been fitted and there have been various other detail improvements in body furniture during the production run of the type. Many Ms now carry tachographs to enable their use on LT tendered routes and private hire work.

In 1987 a programme was put in hand to convert 115 Leaside District Metrobuses to an air braking system. The work was carried out by SBG Engineering at Marine Works, Edinburgh. The programme involved most Metrobuses at Wood Green and Tottenham garages. The rest of the Metrobus fleet has since followed suit. Several Metrobuses at Hounslow were fitted with continuous fluorescent lighting in the upper deck and staircase area during the autumn of 1988.

A number of Ms have been withdrawn as a result of fire and accident damage, including seven which were destroyed by a fire at Southall garage (since closed) on Christmas Day 1985. Thirteen other vehicles involved in this incident were repaired by MCW and returned to service. M 759 was extensively damaged by fire at Enfield on 1st March 1986, Ms 735 and 986 were scrapped following another arson incident at Enfield on 16th April 1988, and M 105 was written off in September 1988 following fire damage whilst working from Norbiton. M 50 was scrapped in November 1992 as a result of fire damage. M 599 is currently being inspected following fire damage at Sutton in March 1993.

In April 1989 M 1069 appeared in a special historical-style London United livery to mark the inauguration of the new Units. After running from Fulwell garage, it moved to Stamford Brook.

Ms 1045, 1398 and 1437 were fitted with Voith D854 four-speed gearboxes during 1987, and were further modified with high-back bus seats in 1988. M 1437 was also fitted with a Gardner turbocharged 240bhp engine in early 1989 and modified to DP43/24F configuration, the central doorway being removed. M 1248, 1367/79/92/3/6 also received four-speed gearboxes in 1988. Ms 1003, 1251, 1367/79/93/6, 1432 are others to have received high-back seating. Ms 804, 1080, 1393/6, 1437 have been converted to single-door, and M 804 has been further converted to open-top.

A number of Metrobuses have received undated registrations from Routemasters. Of these, M 845 surrendered 545 CLT in February 1993 and was re-registered OGK 708Y.

Three Mk2 Metrobuses were ordered by London Transport for its Alternative Vehicle Evaluation trials during 1984/5. Two of these were delivered, becoming M 1441/2. M 1441 had a Gardner 6LXB engine coupled to a Voith D851 gearbox whilst M 1442 had a Cummins L10 engine paired to a Maxwell gearbox. They were delivered in July 1984 and entered service later that year at Stockwell. Both are now at Croydon and have been substantially rebuilt.

As a result of route tendering during 1987, a need arose for additional Metrobuses. Five single-door vehicles surplus to the needs of Greater Manchester and four (including two with Alexander bodywork) which were available from Yorkshire Rider, formerly West Yorkshire PTE, were acquired, and their destination displays modified for LBL use before entering service at Potters Bar. Those from Manchester now work at Enfield.

A further five single-door Metrobuses were acquired from Busways Travel (formerly Tyne & Wear) in the spring of 1988 and placed in service at Potters Bar. Four remain there (having worked from Holloway for a year from July 1989), but M 1485 was sold in February 1992 following fire damage.

Twenty-nine Mk2 Metrobuses (M 1452-80) were leased in 1987/8 for LT services at Harrow Weald. These were withdrawn upon expiry of lease in 1990/91 and returned to dealers, whence they have been widely-dispersed, including 15 which now operate for Reading.

Most Ms are now being upgraded to revised environmental standards, including the fitting of Gardner 6LXDT engines, and are receiving touch-sensitive equipment to their central doorways.

T

In the early 1970s, British Leyland started development of an advanced design of double-decker bus, code-named B15, to which London Transport engineers contributed a number of ideas. In 1975, a number of prototypes of the bus were built for demonstration and test purposes, and prototypes 004 and 005 worked from Chalk Farm between 1975 and 1978. A total of 250 Titans (as the type was christened) were ordered for 1978/9 delivery and another 250 for 1979/80.

T 1 was delivered on 16th August 1978 and the first vehicles entered service on 4th December 1978 when six Ts were allocated to Hornchurch garage.

During 1979 it was announced that because of the poor productivity and high costs and losses at the Park Royal factory, it would be closed from June 1980. The first 250 Titans for LT were completed, some using parts from orders which had been cancelled by other operators, but the other order for 1979/80 delivery fell into abeyance, 100 vehicles being transferred to MCW's Metrobus.

In December 1979 it was announced that production of the Titan would be transferred to Leyland's Cumbria factory. A pre-production run of 13 vehicles was constructed, the first three having Park Royal parts and the other ten some Park Royal materials. These were delivered to LT intermittently during 1981. The production vehicles, starting with T 264 in May, were delivered concurrently. The revised order for 150 vehicles was completed in 1981 and subsequent orders were placed up to T 1125. The last to arrive was T 1096 on 25th November 1984, by which time a decision had been taken to phase the Titan out of production.

Ts 1-100 entered service with automatic fare collection equipment which reduced their seating to 66, whilst Ts 101-797 were delivered without this equipment and seated 68. Ts from 798 upwards had been delivered as 70-seaters, lacking a faretable holder on the nearside of the lower saloon, and a programme started to upseat Ts 1-798 to the same capacity. However, following the end of overhauls at Aldenham this programme was transferred to garages and has not been completed, so that Titans with a mixture of 66, 68 or 70 seats may be found.

The standard engine for the Titan is the Gardner 6LXB unit, although T 261 was delivered with a Leyland TL11 engine and T 345 with a turbocharged L11 version. Later trials saw T 876-80 fitted with TL11 engines and T 881-885 with turbocharged L11 engines. The survivors have been converted to Gardner units.

T 1-263 have non-spigoted wheels, whereas later buses have spigoted wheels. T 676 upwards were delivered with Clayton Dewandre brakes following trials with T 257; earlier Titans have brakes by Automotive Products. Like the Metrobuses, these differences led to segregation of allocations for several years. T 369 was equipped with air braking early in 1989 and a general programme followed to modify other members of the class, being completed early in 1993.

T 765 has a hydraulic driver's seat, as well as a facility for all the front blinds to be changed from the cab. Several Titans have been equipped with tachographs for use on LT tendered services and private hire. Many Titans continue to be converted to fixed front upper-deck windows instead of the original opening type.

Ts 557 and 1000 were fitted with Capital Radio on the upper deck during 1988, and T 929 received dot matrix destination and number displays at front and rear during the autumn of 1988. T 1000 has since also received dot matrix displays.

A fire in the yard of Barking garage on 29th August 1981 destroyed Ts 150 and 206; both were broken up during 1983. Following fire damage in October 1985, T 817 was written off in August 1987 and its remains used for spares. On 10th December 1987 a fire at Sidcup garage (now closed) destroyed Ts 734 and 758 and seriously damaged Ts 708 and 900, and all four were scrapped during 1988. T 512 was severely damaged by fire on 20th March 1988 and was converted to open-top.

T 1039 was withdrawn overturning in an accident at Vauxhall Cross on 17th April 1991, and T 1069 was scrapped during 1991 after catching fire whilst returning from air-brake modifications in the North of England. T 803 and T 998 have become further open-top conversions as a result of serious accident damage.

During 1984, LT acquired five Titans which were surplus to the needs of West Midlands PTE. New in 1978/9, these were numbered T 1126-30. T 1126-9 were licensed early in 1985 for use as type trainers, but from April 1985 all five were upgraded to coach specification at Aldenham Works and allocated to Plumstead and Camberwell garages for use on the 177 Express and private hire work. In March 1987 they were displaced from the 177 by new Olympians and T 1128 moved to Hornchurch garage (since to North Street), the other four remaining in south-east London. All five are still used chiefly as private hire vehicles.

In January 1988 Selkent district received ex-demonstrator BCK 706R on lease from Ensign. Ironically, this had previously been used at Chalk Farm for proving trials on route 24 during 1978. It was numbered T 1131 and formally taken into stock on 28th February 1989. It was sold in May 1993.

Disposal of the T class started in earnest during the autumn of 1992, largely-instigated by tendering losses, and 120 vehicles are in course of sale to Merseybus, with another 150 passing to Ensign (dealer). Most examples of the type have been removed from London Northern, and those in South London are now being replaced by Metrobuses as the opportunity arises, leaving the type generally concentrated in East London, London Central, Selkent and Stanwell Buses. A handful are however allocated for private hire and schools work in Leaside, whilst others at Leaside have been converted as permanent trainers and have received unofficial TT type codes. T 63, 80 and 1063 have been converted to single-door format.

L

During 1983 LT placed orders for three Leyland Olympians to be used alongside equal numbers of MCW Metrobus MkIIs, Dennis Dominators and Volvo Ailsa B55s under the Alternative Vehicle Evaluation programme. The Olympians were the first type to arrive, in February 1984, and L 1 was licensed for service at Stockwell from 23rd March 1984. Their Eastern Coach Works bodies introduced some features unusual to London, including rear-facing seats over the lower saloon rear axle and a nearside route blind at the bottom of the front bay. L 1 is fitted with a Leyland TL11 engine coupled to a Hydracyclic gearbox whilst Ls 2 and 3 have Gardner 6LXB engines coupled to Voith D851 gearboxes.

In June 1985 London Buses placed an order for 260 further Olympians with Eastern Coach Works bodies and Gardner 6LXB engines coupled to Hydracyclic gearboxes for delivery in 1986/7. They incorporated certain Ogle Designs features including straight staircase, split-entrance steps, three-step exit, new-style handrails with bright green covering, and 'Bus Stopping' signs in both saloons activated by the bell push. Delivery of this order commenced on 27th January 1986. The first two were delivered to Chiswick, but all subsequent arrivals inaugurated a new policy of delivery direct to host garages in the intended operating units. The first entered service at Plumstead on 22nd March 1986. Subsequent route tendering specifying the use of newer vehicles has led to widespread movements of the type, though they remain confined to their original operating areas.

L 166-171 were delivered with high-back seating for use on route X68 at Norwood. L 260-3 followed similarly-upgraded for use on the 177 Express (since replaced by express journeys on 53) at Plumstead. The latter quartet also appear on other work including private hire and long-distance routes to the seaside (in the summer) or major shopping centres; L 261 now works from New Cross.

Twenty-eight further Olympians (L 264-291), this time with Northern Counties single-door bodywork, were leased for Bexleybus services from January 1988. They were withdrawn upon expiry of lease in 1990/1 and returned to dealers, whence they have been widely-dispersed, many now operating for Tyne & Wear. Another 23 Olympians (L 292-314) were ordered with Leyland bodywork following the successful tender for LT route 237 from Stamford Brook garage from 8th January 1990. All of these have Cummins units and carry 'Riverside Bus' fleetnames. The last three have high-back seating and were used for the short-lived Airbus service A3 to Stansted Airport during the summer of 1991.

Forty further Olympians with Alexander dual-door bodywork were delivered to Leaside in the spring of 1992, the last four having high-back seats. All have been placed in service at Stamford Hill alongside Metrobuses.

V

London Transport ordered three Volvo Ailsa B55 buses with Alexander bodywork as part of the Alternative Vehicle Evaluation trials. Vs 1 and 2 were delivered on 18th April 1984 and entered service at Stockwell during the summer of that year.

V 3 was delivered on 6th June and featured an experimental design with a second door at the rear instead of at the centre and a second staircase at the back. It did not enter service until 18th March 1985 and was used on crewed routes as it was not possible to obtain agreement for its use on an opo basis.

All three buses were taken out of service at the end of August 1986 and stored. During October they were moved to Potters Bar, where Vs 1 and 2 entered service in December. V 3 was modified for opo use by the removal of the rear doorway and its seating was revised from H36/28D to H38/30F, although retaining the rear staircase. Thus modified, it entered service at the end of February 1987. An accident in October 1992 led to its withdrawal, though it has subsequently been sold through dealers to Black Prince of Morley, with whom it is likely to re-enter service.

Sixty-two secondhand Volvo Ailsas were acquired from South Yorkshire PTE and West Midlands Travel in 1987/8. These have all since been withdrawn and sold.

S

London Buses ordered nine Scania N112DRB double-deckers during the summer of 1989 with single-door Alexander bodywork to standard RH-type design (with some adjustments) for LT tendered route 263 from Potters Bar garage. The order was fulfilled in July 1989 and the type entered service on 29th July.

A further 20 similar vehicles (S 10-29) entered service towards the end of 1991, initially at West Ham garage (since closed), including several painted in dedicated livery for Docklands Express service D1. Shortly afterwards, in December 1991, two more Scanias with Northern Counties bodywork (S 30/1) entered service at Potters Bar to cater for increased requirements on the 263. All of these were based on the upgraded N113DRB chassis.

In the spring of 1992 the two Northern Counties vehicles moved to East London in exchange for two of the 1991 batch of Alexanders, and in the summer of 1992 nine further Alexander-bodied vehicles were sent to Holloway, where they were repainted in a special livery for 'Red Route' X43.

A further 40 Northern Counties-bodied Scanias (S 32-71) were delivered from June to October 1992 for use in East London at Upton Park and Bow.

VC

A successful bid for LT tendered route 133 during 1989 resulted in an order for 27 Volvo Citybuses with Northern Counties bodywork. The first arrived on 5th November 1989 and delivery was completed on 5th January 1990. These vehicles entered service on 6th January 1990. Like the S class, they are very much to standard design with minor modifications for London requirements. The first three have high-back seating throughout, and the next three have high-back seating in the upper saloon only.

A further 11 were received during 1990 for tendered route 196, which was gained from 28th April 1990. A further example arrived at the end of December 1991 to cater for increased needs.

All 39 vehicles operate from Stockwell garage, and many of them have received undated registrations transferred from Routemasters.

SP

The new Optare Spectra design of double-decker, based on DAF running units, elicited speedy interest from London Buses when it was announced in 1991, and 25 vehicles were delivered from 4th September 1992. Twenty-four of these were specified as single-door vehicles and allocated to London Central for the opo conversion of route 3 from 2nd January 1993, first entering service four weeks earlier on route 40 on a temporary basis. Delivery was completed on 20th February 1993.

The other (SP 2) was built to dual-door design for Metroline, to whom it was delivered on 18th September 1992, entering service on 8th October at Cricklewood garage on routes 16/A. During March 1993 SP 2 was reallocated to Camberwell and will eventually be converted to single-door format after evaluation with other subsidiaries.

RT/RV

A single example of the RT class remains on books. RT 1530, now allocated to Stanwell Buses, was overhauled and repainted during 1992 by BEL Engineering, and is now in store pending future developments.

Newly-gained school contracts at Stamford Hill from May 1991 entailed the transfer of four Fleetlines into this garage. To support them, a 1966 AEC Regent V with Park Royal bodywork was acquired from Wealden PSV of Five Oak Green, Kent and classified RV 1. Originally new to East Kent, this vehicle had previously seen service on London sightseeing tours with Obsolete Fleet from November 1981 until June 1982. It was then used by Pardes House School, Finchley for a further two years before returning to Kent. It is now used for private hire work, training duties and schools work, but has never entered normal revenue service.

LS

Six Leyland Nationals were ordered in 1972 to run alongside Metro-Scanias with a view to evaluating future orders for single-deckers. The Leyland Nationals were 10.3-metre vehicles of B36D+27 type. All entered service at Dalston garage (since closed) on route S2 on 29th November 1973. They were followed by another 431 Nationals between 1975 and 1979.

During 1980, sixty-nine 10.6-metre Leyland National 2s were ordered to convert the Red Arrow network from MBA and SMS operation. These have Leyland 0680 11.1-litre engines coupled to Hydracyclic gearboxes rather than pneumocyclic. LS 438 arrived in December 1980 and the batch was completed on 2nd July 1981. Seating was restricted to the rear portion and to bench seats over the front axle, maximising standing accommodation.

Following reductions in the Red Arrow network from 4th September 1982, a number of Mk2 vehicles were surplus to requirements. LS 457 was fitted with a ZF gearbox at Chiswick before re-entering service, but other spare LSs were gradually converted to standard bus capacity of B36D over a period of time and placed in service at Stockwell on route P4.

During 1984, LS 454 was fitted with a Ratcliffe wheelchair lift in the centre doorway for use on new Mobility Bus services in the Stratford and Walthamstow area. In 1985 LSs 356/96 were converted to similar configuration with improved chair clamps. A similar conversion was carried out on LS 105 by PMT Engineering in the autumn of 1986. In the summer of 1987 nine further surplus LSs were formally transferred to LRT ownership and sent to MCW for conversion to Mobility Buses. Six were then leased back to London Buses for use on new Mobility Bus services from Peckham and Cricklewood garages, and the other three were hired to Kentish Bus from 17th October 1989. The earlier examples also passed into formal LRT ownership, remaining with LBL. Additional Mobility Bus vehicles were converted from two 11.3-metre Leyland Nationals provided by Southdown and Hastings Buses, becoming LSL 1 (WYJ 165S) and LSL 2 (RUF 42R) in November 1990 and July 1991 respectively. LSL 2 went on lease to Kentish Bus, never entering service with London Buses, and the subsequent loss of some Mobility Bus networks by LBL under tendering has reduced this element of the fleet to three LSs at each of Peckham and North Street.

In July 1985 the upseated Mk2 vehicles became surplus when route P4 was lost under tendering. After most had been overhauled, all 13 were moved to Holloway for route 210 from 21st June 1986. In 1987/8 they were returned to the Red Arrow fleet to meet an increased requirement following the introduction of new routes, but most remained as 36-seaters and were interworked alongside the standee vehicles on all Red Arrow routes. LS 491 received a dot-matrix destination display during 1989.

Subsequent reductions in the Red Arrow network led to some Mk2 vehicles again being stored, including most (but not all) of the 36-seaters. Ten have been converted to B44F and sent to Uxbridge for use on route 607 and big bus journeys on the U1.

Eighteen standard LSs were set aside in the summer of 1989 for new Docklands Shuttle services. In the event, only 11 were required; LS 7, 35, 88, 97, 123/77, 277/45/59, 395, 411 were fitted with headrests by Hants & Dorset Engineering and painted into a special livery, entering service on route D5 on Mondays to Fridays and also on D3 on Saturdays from 30th June 1991. They were withdrawn from this work during 1992 and most have now been transferred to Stanwell Buses.

Other than those used by Stanwell Buses (Westlink) or as Mobility Buses, all standard LSs have now been withdrawn from regular service, and most sold. Westlink's LS 431 received a special livery for the centenary of Surrey County Council in July 1989 and still carries this.

GLS

The National Greenway project, designed to inject new life into older Leyland Nationals with a reasonable life-expectancy, engaged the interest of London Buses when it was announced, and LS 466 was sent away as a trial conversion, returning in October 1992 as GLS 1. It entered service on Red Arrow routes early in December 1992, and a further 41 such conversions are now to be undertaken. CentreWest also received GLS 2, rebuilt from former Crosville/North Western 11.6-metre Leyland National Mk2 FCA 9X. This has entered service alongside LSs and LXs on the 607 at Uxbridge, and was re-registered to 292 CLT in February 1993.

LX

Two Leyland Lynx buses were purchased by the London Borough of Hillingdon at the end of December 1988 and leased to LBL for use on routes 128/A at Uxbridge, forming the LX class. Both are painted in a similar livery to the three LSs previously employed on this work. Nominally to bus specification, the rearmost 14 seats have high backs.

Whilst not originally intended as experimental vehicles, it proved convenient to bring both vehicles into trials conducted from 1989 to assess future single-deck requirements. They were joined by six further Lynxes delivered during September 1989 for tendered route 283, entering service from Shepherd's Bush garage on 14th September and moving to Stamford Brook, where they received Riverside Bus names, on 5th January 1990.

Three further Lynxes were purchased from Merthyr Tydfil in December 1989 for use on the 128/A, replacing the LSs which had been held as spares; all of these received undated registrations from Routemasters, and were, like the first two, owned by the London Borough of Hillingdon.

Those on the 283 were displaced by Dennis Darts in February 1991 and translated to the 190. The Uxbridge vehicles were withdrawn from the 128/A on 17th August 1991 and after being repainted and fitted with high-back seating throughout were formally transferred to LBL ownership and deployed on the 607 route.

LA/LN

Selkent received a batch of 16 Dennis Lance single-deckers with Alexander dual-door bodywork for the opo conversion from Catford garage of route 36B on weekdays from 31st May 1992. The choice of single-deckers was partly influenced by a desire to overcome vandalism problems on double-deckers, though capacity problems quickly meant that the LAs stayed garage-bound on Sundays, when Titans still have to be used on the 36B.

The satisfactory performance of the Lance led to a further order for 31 to be delivered in the spring of 1993. Bodied by Northern Counties, these are being allocated to Metroline for use on routes 113 and 302, entering service from 24th April 1993.

VN

An order was placed towards the end of 1992 for 13 Volvo B10B single-deckers with Northern Counties bodywork for use at Stockwell on route 88, converted to opo as recently as August 1992. Delivery started in the spring of 1993 and the type entered service from 15th May 1993.

DA

Two Optare Delta buses on DAF chassis were ordered for use in single-deck experimental trials following the demonstration visit of demonstrator F370BUA on the 180 at Plumstead during mid-March 1989. They appeared at the British Coach Rally at Southampton on 22nd/23rd April 1989. DA 1 was a B49F vehicle, and was formally delivered on 6th June 1989 with ex-Routemaster registration WLT400. It entered service on 30th June 1989 at Bromley as a private hire vehicle, moving to Plumstead in February 1991. In November 1992 it was re-registered F802NGY and moved to Seven Kings. Following the closure of Seven Kings garage on 20th March 1993, DA 1 has moved to Stanwell Buses.

DA 2 was delivered on 15th June 1989 to B30D Red Arrow specification and was licensed from 1st September 1989. It saw only limited use before being converted to B49F and sent to Stanwell Buses in May 1990.

Seven further Deltas were delivered in the spring of 1990 for Stanwell Buses to use on tendered route 110 from 28th April. They are in full Westlink livery.

Optare Delta demonstrator G684KNW was used at Seven Kings from May 1990 and eventually taken into stock in August 1991, becoming DA10. It was followed by 19 further Deltas delivered to Seven Kings between April and June 1992. Following the closure of Seven Kings garage on 20th March 1993 these vehicles have all moved to Barking for use on routes 169 and 369. Another six were received in April and May 1993 for route 150 at Barking.

LLW/SSW

Increasing demand to provide vehicles suitable for access by the disabled led to orders being placed towards the end of 1992 for 68 low-floor vehicles. Thirty-eight of these will be based on Dennis Lance chassis and the other 30 on Scania N113CRL chassis, all having Wright Pathfinder 320 bodywork.

Delivery is due to start in summer 1993. The LLW class will be allocated to London United (route 120), Metroline (route 186) and CentreWest (route 222), whilst the SLWs will go to East London (routes undecided) and Leaside (route 144A).

DARTS

The Dennis 'Dart' was demonstrated to London Buses at the turn of 1989/1990, and an initial order was placed for 57 vehicles on 8.5-metre chassis, forming the DT class. The first 27 have Duple bodywork for use on midibus routes based at Richmond and Hounslow, entering service at Fulwell garage on 7th April 1990 and from Hounslow three weeks later. The other 30 have Carlyle bodies and were initially used on midibus conversions in the Bromley area during the summer of 1990.

Such was the success of the type that a further 110 DTs were delivered over the next year, enabling further conversions (often as a result of LT tendering) at Fulwell, Thornton Heath, Willesden, Edgware, Harrow Weald, Hounslow and Stamford Brook. One of the original demonstrators also came into stock as DT 168, receiving a Routemaster registration.

The availability of the Dennis Dart with bodywork by other manufacturers was quickly seized upon by LBL when it was announced. The DW class, bodied by Wright on 8.5-metre chassis, started to arrive in November 1990 with an initial batch of 91 vehicles, and entered service at Alperton, Westbourne Park, Wood Green, Catford and Sutton. All of these had Belfast registrations except for those at Sutton. A further demonstrator was initially allocated fleet number DW 00 before being taken into stock as DW 100 in May 1991, and another 20 DWs were delivered to Westbourne Park to complete the conversion of routes 28 and 31 from MA operation in the late summer of 1991. Fourteen further DWs arrived at Westbourne Park for route 70 in the spring of 1992, and another six went to Merton in November 1992 for midibus conversions. Another 38 were delivered in February and March 1993 for use in the revised Barking and Ilford network at Barking and North Street garages from 20th March 1993.

The DW class has also appeared on 9-metre chassis. Fourteen vehicles were received at the end of 1990 and sent to Stanwell Buses for use on the tendered 371 group at Kingston, forming the DWL class. A further 12 DWLs were delivered to Barking for route 62 in February 1993.

Reeve Burgess bodywork was chosen for a batch of 52 Darts on 8.5-metre chassis delivered during the spring of 1991 as the DR class for use at Hounslow, Streatham (since moved to Norwood), Merton and Stockwell in connection with the Wandsworth Area Route Network scheme introduced on 25th May 1991. In practice the Hounslow examples intermix with the DT allocation there. Only the first 19 were built by Reeve Burgess at Chesterfield, the remaining 33 being sub-contracted to the parent Plaxton factory at Scarborough. An extra three arrived from Plaxton in August 1991, completing an exercise designed to rationalise the allocation of midibus types in the light of changing needs. Further batches of DRs for London United, Metroline and London General have taken the class total up to 153.

The most recent Dart variant is based on the 9-metre chassis as the DRL class, bodied by Plaxton. Sixteen entered service at Peckham on route P11 in September and October 1991, releasing SRs for use elsewhere; the first four were named after characters in the locally-based BBC sitcom "Only Fools and Horses". Further batches of DRLs have been delivered for use at Chalk Farm, Wood Green, Victoria Basement and Hounslow, with more on order which will take the total of Darts in the fleet to 681, an impressive total in just three years.

BL

An order for 95 Bristol LHs with Eastern Coach Works 39-seat bodies to 7ft 6in width was placed in November 1974 following inspection of a Hants & Dorset LH at Chiswick in 1973. The first vehicles arrived in February 1976 and entered service from North Street garage during April 1976.

The BL class was gradually reduced during the 1980s and the last examples ran on route 251 at Edgware in January 1991. Most of the surplus vehicles were sold over the years, though BL 36 and BL 81 were adapted as coaches in 1986 and 1987 respectively. New legislation relating to driver training vehicles enabled a stay of execution for the survivors in 1991, and they were readily adapted for this purpose by Centrewest and London United, although those with London United are now being withdrawn.

MINIBUSES AND MIDIBUSES

Minibuses first entered service with London Transport in 1972 when, at the request of the GLC, four minibus routes were introduced to serve roads in the suburbs where full sized buses were felt not to be justified. Sixteen Ford Transits with Strachans Pacemaker 16-seater bodywork were taken into stock to operate these and were classified FS. All four original routes (B1, C11, P4, W9) eventually graduated to larger vehicles though two other FS routes led to further deliveries of the type up to November 1985, when FS 27-29 arrived. The type came out of scheduled service in June 1989 when the H2 route was lost to R&I Tours under tendering. The sole survivor is now used as a staff bus by Westlink.

Two Dodge S56 vehicles with Rootes bodywork were delivered as the A class in January 1983 for route PB1 at Potters Bar. They were taken out of use on 21st June 1986 when the route was transferred to North Mymms Coaches. After being used as spares for other minibus routes A 1 was relegated to training work on 22nd November 1988. A 2 was stored in October 1988 and sold in April 1990 after extended loan to Willesden Technical College. A 1 remains in stock.

During 1986 LRT finalised plans for a midibus network based on Orpington and LBL successfully gained the tenders for six midibus routes. An order was placed for 24 Iveco Daily vehicles with Robin Hood bodywork, three of them with dual-purpose seating, and five Optare City Pacers, the latter design breaking new ground in being a purpose-built minibus rather than a conversion of a parcel van body.

The Ivecos were delivered from 27th June 1986 as the RH class and twenty were allocated to the Orpington Buses subsidiary, trading as 'Roundabout'. Others saw use on Chelsea Hoppa service C3 and at Bexleyheath. The type is now reduced to four spares at Orpington, the remainder being sold.

The five City Pacers entered service at Orpington on 16th August 1986 as the OV class and had five-speed manual gearboxes. A further 19 were introduced on new route C1 at Victoria Basement from 25th October 1986. Twenty-five similar vehicles (but having semi-automatic gearboxes) were delivered to LRT and leased to London Country North West for use on route C2 from March 1987. From 25th June 1988 this route together with operation of the vehicles was taken over by LBL. All have now been taken out of service and sold. OV 2 was donated to the London Transport Museum in the summer of 1991.

A further three City Pacers were delivered in January and February 1988 for use on the Carelink service from 21st March 1988, linking Victoria to other mainline stations and connecting with Airbus services to Heathrow Airport at Victoria. They reverted to LT ownership in October 1992 and passed to Thorpe, NW10.

As a result of the introduction of Chelsea Harbour Hoppa route C3 from 13th April 1987 two Freight Rover Sherpa minibuses with Carlyle Works conversions were received in dark blue livery and classified SC. SC 2 was returned to Carlyle (dealer) in March 1989, but SC 1 remains in stock, now relegated to driver training.

Twenty-two MCW Metroriders were allocated to the Stanwell Buses fleet as the MR class for use on routes K1/2/3 from 27th June 1987, painted in Westlink colours. The last four were specified with high-back seating for occasional use on private hire work. A further 30 vehicles were ordered for use at Harrow Weald from 14th November 1987, painted in Harrow Buses livery of red skirt, cream lower panels and red upperwork. They were later displaced by SRs and moved to other schemes. Another 24 were ordered in connection with the Bexleybus network introduced on 16th January 1988. Twelve of these introduced the lengthened Metrorider design to London. Classified MRL, they were delivered to Orpington in January 1988.

During the summer of 1988, a further sixteen MRLs were received, fifteen for use by Westlink and an extra vehicle for Orpington. The Westlink vehicles released earlier MRs for use elsewhere and these are now well-scattered, as are most of the other earlier Metroriders, displaced by larger vehicles or by the loss of tendered routes.

From 5th August 1988 LBL introduced services G1 and G2 to serve St George's Hospital, Tooting, and six more MRs were delivered to Streatham Garage. These are owned by Wandsworth Health Authority, and entered service with fleet numbers SG 1-6 before being altered to MR 93-8 later in August 1988.

A further order for seven MRs and 28 MRLs was placed for the autumn of 1988. Most of these were in connection with the Walthamstow scheme introduced on 29th October 1988 and 4th March 1989, although some of the MRLs were held back for use at Clapton garage from 27th May 1989.

Westlink received MCW demonstrator D482NOX on extended hire in February 1988 and this passed formally into stock from December 1988 as MR 134.

MRL 135 was delivered in July 1990 for use at Sutton. This vehicle featured an improved passenger circulation area at the entrance, resulting in downseating to 26 seats, and was constructed by Optare at Leeds following the closure of the MCW plant at Birmingham. A further 24 MRLs to this design were received towards the end of 1990, allowing upgrading of the Bexleyheath fleet and the introduction of new routes from Plumstead.

At this point it had not been intended to purchase further Metroriders, but another 50 were ordered in the spring of 1991, going to Bromley and London General. Those with London General contributed towards the withdrawal of the OV class from route C1, whilst those at Bromley released Dennis Darts for use elsewhere.

Further orders have been received for 12 MRLs (used at Holloway on tendered routes W4 and W5 from the turn of 1991/2) and 20 MRLs in the spring of 1993 for London General, London Northern and London Central. These take the class total to 241.

Withdrawals of Metroriders started in the spring of 1992.

Four Optare StarRiders, an elongated version of the City Pacer concept based on Mercedes-Benz 811D chassis with seating for up to 33 passengers, were ordered for new route L3 between Downham Health Centre and Catford from 29th July 1988. They were allocated to Catford garage as the SR class and carried a black cat logo. SR 4 has a dot matrix destination display. A further 24 SRs were delivered to Peckham for tendered routes P11, P12 and P13 from 19th November 1988, and another 25 were completed in March 1989, entering service at Walthamstow on route 211, Victoria Basement on route C2, and at New Cross for the 286. Most of the Walthamstow examples moved to Bow on 24th February 1990.

Six further SRs were delivered to Bexleyheath in July 1989, followed by further batches of 22 (mostly for further minibus routes from Catford garage), 24 (to replace MRs at Harrow Weald), 16 (to complete the conversion of the C2 at Victoria Basement), and an extra two to cater for increased demand on the 286, arriving in January 1990.

SR 10 suffered fire damage in February 1990 and was scrapped. Like the MRs and MRLs, allocations of the SRs have become more widely-distributed as a result of changing requirements since their delivery.

To service new route E5 which started on 26th November 1989 between Havelock Estate and Greenford under the 'Southall Shuttle' banner, five Mercedes-Benz 709D minibuses with Reeve Burgess bodywork were received, forming the MT class. All are fitted with rear wheelchair lifts, and are painted in red livery with a broad white band on each side. Another two arrived in August 1989 to meet increased demand. These last two were transferred to Mobility Bus services from Uxbridge during July 1991. A further MT, based on the longer 811D chassis, was received during the spring of 1989 for use as a dual-control training vehicle at Catford, moving to Plumstead in January 1991. It is also available for private hire work and is fitted with a manual five-speed gearbox, tinted glass and soft trim; a courier seat, provided at the front of the vehicle, can be used by driving instructors or private hire guides. In June 1991 this vehicle was reclassified MTL 6.

A further Mercedes-Benz on 811D chassis arrived in December 1989 and entered service at Uxbridge as MTL 1. Another was used at Westbourne Park, initially as a demonstrator before being taken into stock in November 1990 as MTL 2. Three further MTLs arrived in December 1990 on extended loan from the manufacturers. MTL 3 and 4 have subsequently passed into LBL ownership. The MTL type can currently be found at Bexleyheath and Catford.

Plans to convert routes 28 and 31 to high-frequency midibus operation were announced during 1988. Seventy Mercedes-Benz 811D vehicles with Alexander 28-seat bodywork were ordered, featuring special accommodation for luggage and a wide entrance area to facilitate rapid loading. A further 37 vehicles were added to the order to provide a fleet for the Uxbridge U-Line scheme which was introduced during the spring of 1989. The last seven of the complete order were specified with high-back seating so as to be available for private hire and other duties when appropriate.

Delivery commenced in the autumn of 1988 as the MA class, and some vehicles were used temporarily at Hanwell, Orpington and Victoria Basement. The first of the Uxbridge routes, U4, was introduced on 18th February 1989 to replace the 204, and the 28 was converted from Westbourne Park garage on 4th March 1989, followed by the 31 on 15th April. The rest of the U-Line network was introduced from 27th May 1989. Due to an error at the bodybuilders MA 46-55 were delivered with the registrations intended for MA 95-9/0-4. As a result, new registrations F946-955BMS were taken out for MA 90-99 when these arrived, F646-655XMS being voided, and during April 1989 the relevant vehicles were renumbered so that registrations matched fleet numbers. MA 101 received a Routemaster registration during May 1989. Another 17 MAs were delivered in spring 1990 to convert routes 39/239 from Victoria and Putney, and a further ten in the spring of 1991 for the 265 at Putney.

The original Westbourne Park MAs were displaced by Dennis Darts from the spring of 1991, and all have now been widely-dispersed for use elsewhere. MA 7 is being converted as a Mobility Bus.

During 1988 LRT offered route H20 for tender between Hounslow Civic Centre and Ivybridge Estate. After further discussions the route was instead introduced on 18th March 1989 as a commercial venture between Westlink and the London Borough of Hounslow. Three CVE Omni minibuses, owned by the London Borough of Hounslow, were received to operate the route; they have basic capacity for one wheelchair but can be converted to accommodate another by removal of seven seats. CV 1 and 3 are in white livery whilst CV 2 is in red. A fourth CV was received on 27th November 1989 with suitable equipment for use on the Carelink service from Victoria Basement. It was only used fitfully on this service and in July 1991 was moved to Harrow Weald for use on Mobility Bus services there until returned to LT in December 1992.

A further three CVs arrived in the Stanwell Buses fleet during the spring of 1992 for use on routes R61 and R62 in the Richmond area, jointly-supported by LT and the London Borough of Richmond-upon-Thames.

Carlyle Works provided a demonstrator on Mercedes-Benz 811D chassis from July 1989. This was eventually taken into formal stock during April 1990 at Catford garage as MC 1. Another four arrived in August 1990 for use at Orpington, and MC 1 joined these in April 1991.

Further midibus conversions at Catford from 2nd December 1989 led to the arrival of the MW class of 16 vehicles with Wright bodywork on Mercedes-Benz 811D chassis. These were noteworthy in introducing Northern Ireland registrations to the London fleet. A further demonstrator arrived at the end of 1990, being numbered MW 00 and working from a variety of garages when not required on demonstration outside London, but was returned to Wrights in the autumn of 1991. A further demonstrator, MW 17, arrived on long-term loan at Victoria Basement in the summer of 1992, moving to Uxbridge in March 1993, and 20 further MWs are currently entering service at Potters Bar from April 1993.

Also from Wright's came 90 similar vehicles on Renault 50 chassis for CentreWest for delivery in 1990, forming the RW class. Most were used for the protracted midibus scheme in the Ealing area, but the first 14 entered service when the 282 was converted to midibus from 3rd March 1990.

Midibus conversions in the East End led to a call for 25 vehicles at Bow garage from 24th February 1990, and the RB class of Renault 50s with Reeve Burgess 'Beaver' bodywork was delivered from December 1989 for this purpose. Another eight arrived in October 1990. Two more RBs were demonstrated at Uxbridge and Bow from the end of 1991 for about a year.

A contract for the Department of Health & Social Security from June 1990 led to two Freight Rover Sherpas with Dormobile bodywork being leased from Carlyle Works. These were classified SD and ran from Clapton until July 1991, when they were replaced by MRs and returned to their owners.

The London Borough of Hounslow sponsored new routes H24 and H25 from January 1991 and an order was placed for eight Iveco Daily vehicles with Reeve Burgess bodywork featuring tail lifts and wheelchair facilities. The resultant FR class operates at Hounslow garage in a special livery of white with green relief.

Towards the end of 1992 an order was placed for two Iveco Daily midibuses with Marshall 'C31' bodywork for use at Orpington. The order was subsequently increased to 10 vehicles, entering service from April 1993 as the FM class.

Numerous other minibuses have been hired from time to time during recent years, though less so lately. Some have acted as demonstrators, some as staff buses or as temporary additions to the training fleet, and others have been supplied by dealers on a short-term basis whilst owned vehicles have been returned for modifications or for other reasons.

COACHES

With the privatisation of London Coaches in May 1992, only 22 pure coaches remain with six of the London Buses subsidiaries.

The main type represented is the TPL class of six Leyland Tigers bodied by Plaxton. TPL 1 and 2 were new to Leaside at Wood Green in October 1989, followed by TPL 3 with the former London Forest subsidiary at Leyton in March 1990 and TPL 5 with East London at North Street in November 1990. TPL 7 and 8 were delivered to Leyton in April 1991. The Leyton vehicles moved to East London (North Street) (TPL 3 and 7) and Leaside (Wood Green) (TPL 8) in November 1991. TPL 9 was a secondhand vehicle delivered to Metroline in March 1992 upon the opening of their private hire section, accompanied by LD 5, a secondhand Leyland Leopard with Duple coachwork. TPL 9 was returned to its lessors in March 1993.

Two Leyland Tigers with Duple coachwork were delivered to Metroline in March 1993, forming the TDL class. Other Leylands, this time Leopards with Plaxton coachwork, are LP 5 and 6. Delivered secondhand to London United in June 1989, they were transferred to Leaside in November 1991 and entered service after overhaul and repaint in the spring of 1992.

Eight further coaches are based on DAF chassis. The newest are DV 36-9, bodied by Van Hool and delivered to Plumstead in March 1993. Older examples are DV 67, a 1988 Van Hool-bodied MB230LB615 delivered to Plumstead in February 1992, DD 35/6 based on SB2305DHS585 chassis with Duple bodywork, delivered to Plumstead in January 1992, and DP 1 of 1988 with Plaxton coachwork on identical chassis, delivered to Plumstead in August 1992.

Two Volvo coaches are in stock. VT 1, a 1977 B58-61 vehicle with Duple coachwork, arrived with Stanwell Buses as a training vehicle in June 1991, and VP 1, a B10M-60 of 1990 with Plaxton coachwork, was delivered to Holloway in March 1993.

The final coach, and perhaps the most untypical of London, is SKY 1, a Neoplan Auwaerter Skyliner double-decker of 1988, which has been used by London Northern at Holloway since May 1991.

SERVICE VEHICLES

An organisation the size of London Transport inevitably needs a large number of ancillary vehicles, the most obvious being breakdown tenders for both road and rail vehicles and towing lorries for the road fleet. Other vehicles operated range from estate cars for staff transport (some are dual-pedal control driver-training cars), radio cars for inspectors, minibuses and vans of varying sizes (used for carrying miscellaneous small parts, tickets and publicity material etc) to larger covered and open lorries and articulated vehicles for carrying major items such as engines, traction motors, plant and machinery from works to garages and depots.

From 1980, the heavy vehicle intake has generally been of Ford manufacture, with smaller numbers of Bedford/Vauxhall machines and a phase of Dodges in the first half of the 1980s. Mercedes-Benz vehicles have also found more recent favour. Since mid-1982, all small vehicles up to the size of the Ford Transit have been leased and these are now given a separate number series from 3000 upwards. Owned vehicles continue to use the 2000 series, except that former buses retain their previous numbers, sometimes subtly altered.

The ancillary fleet is administered by the Central Distribution Services subsidiary of London Underground Ltd on behalf of London Transport and its subsidiaries. Some LBL subsidiaries have also taken vehicles into stock independently.

CLASS CODES

Double deckers	DMS	Daimler opo
	DM	Crew-operated version of DMS
	D	DM with modifications for opo use
	L	Leyland Olympian
	M	MCW Metrobus
	RM	Routemaster
	RMA	Routemaster Airways (ex-British Airways)
	RMC	Routemaster Coach
	RML	Routemaster Lengthened
	RV	AEC Regent V
	S	Scania
	SP	Optare Spectra
	T	Leyland Titan
	V	Volvo Ailsa
	VC	Volvo Citybus
Single deckers	BL	Bristol LH
	CV	OMNI/CVE minibus
	DA	Optare Delta
	DR	Dennis Dart (Reeve Burgess/Plaxton body)
	DRL	Lengthened form of DR class
	DT	Dennis Dart (Duple/Carlyle body)
	DW	Dennis Dart (Wright body)
	DWL	Lengthened form of DW class
	FM	Fiat Iveco (Marshall body)
	FR	Fiat Iveco (Reeve Burgess body with tail-lift)
	FS	Ford single-decker
	GLS	Greenway Leyland National
	LA	Dennis Lance (Alexander body)
	LLW	Dennis Lance low-floor (Wright body)
	LN	Dennis Lance (Northern Counties body)
	LS	Leyland National single-decker
	LX	Leyland Lynx single-decker
	MA	Mercedes-Benz (Alexander body)
	MC	Mercedes-Benz (Carlyle body)
	MR	MCW Metrorider
	MRL	MCW/Optare Metrorider lengthened
	MT	Mercedes-Benz (Reeve Burgess body with tail-lift)
	MTL	Lengthened form of MT
	MW	Mercedes-Benz (Wright body)
	RB	Renault (Reeve Burgess body)
	RH	Robin Hood minibus
	RW	Renault (Wright body)
	SC	Freight Rover Sherpa minibus (Carlyle body)
	SLW	Scania low-floor (Wright body)
	SR	Optare StarRider midibus
	VN	Volvo (Northern Counties body)
Coaches	DD	DAF (Duple body)
	DP	DAF (Plaxton body)
	DV	DAF (Van Hool body)
	LD	Leyland Leopard (Duple body)
	LP	Leyland Leopard (Plaxton body)
	SKY	Auwerter Neoplan Skyliner
	TDL	Leyland Tiger (Duple body) lengthened
	TPL	Leyland Tiger (Plaxton body) lengthened
	VP	Volvo (Plaxton body)
	VT	Volvo (Duple body) for training

Above **RM644 was converted to open-top for London Coaches in July 1988. It became the only open-top RM to have passed on to another LBL subsidiary when it moved to Metroline in December 1991. When found at Waterloo in August 1992 it was on loan to London Central for a regular summer roster on route 12.** Tony Wilson

Above Right **The separation of the northern end of the 159 as new route 139 in March 1992 led to several RMs being brought out of the reserve fleet, as well as the reintroduction of crewed work at Chalk Farm garage. RM446 crosses Trafalgar Square, showing the route branding now common on several Routemaster-worked services.** Tony Wilson

Right **Holloway's route 10 is another treated to route branding. The main allocation is with RMLs, with just a handful of standard RMs providing support. The passing point 'Hyde Park' is added on the RMLs, appearing over the half-width window. RM2136 passes between King's Cross and St Pancras Stations.** Russell Upcraft

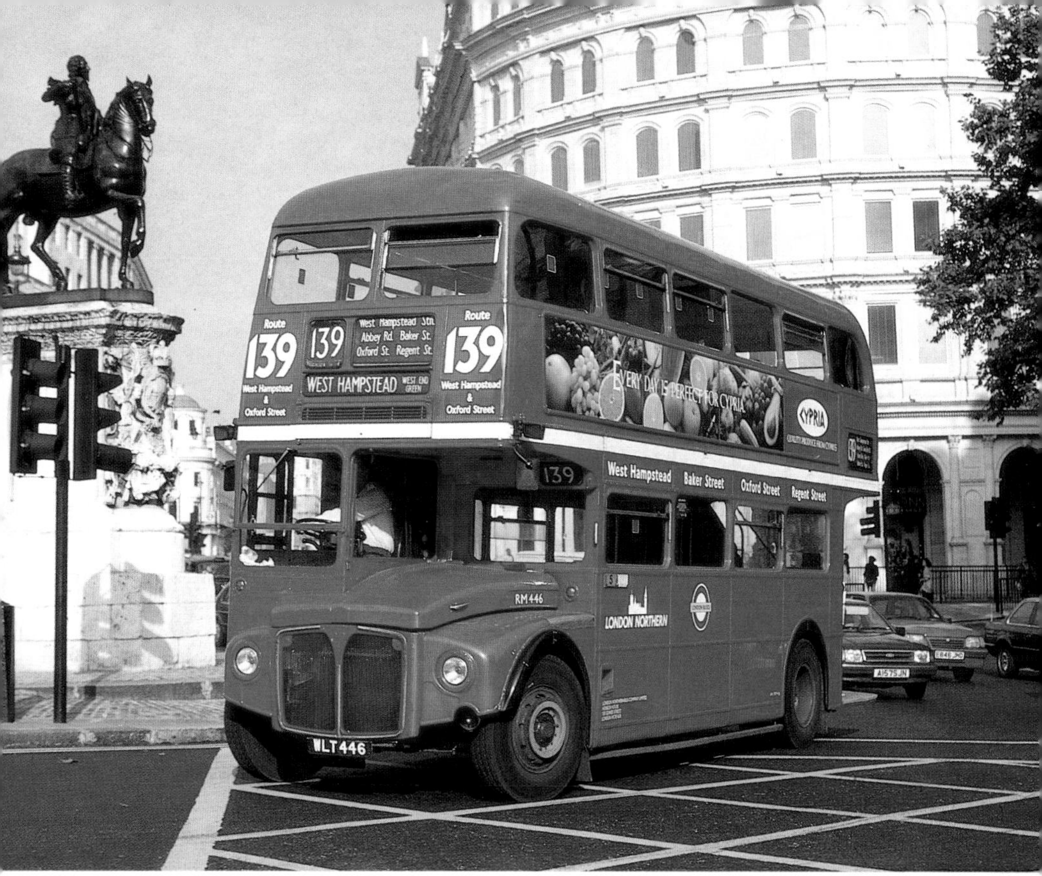
Route
139
West Hampstead
&
Oxford Street
139
West Hampstead Stn.
Abbey Rd. Baker St.
Oxford St. Regent St.
WEST HAMPSTEAD
WEST END GREEN
EVERY DAY IS PERFECT FOR CYPRIA
CYPRIA
139
West Hampstead
Baker Street
Oxford Street
Regent Street
RM446
LONDON NORTHERN
WLT446

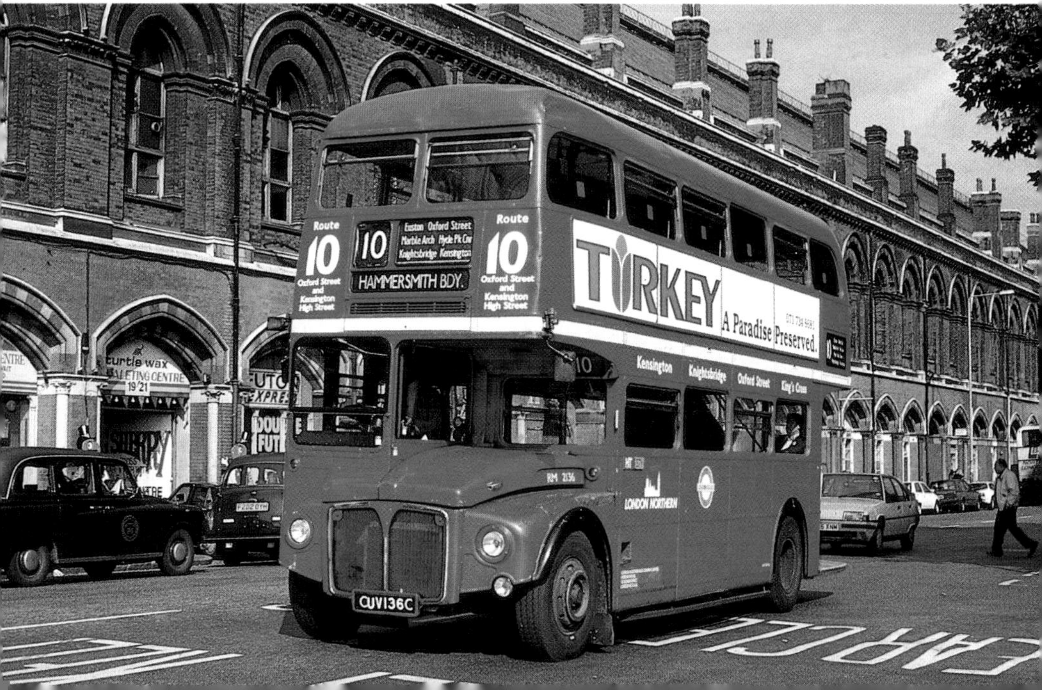
turtle wax
VALETING CENTRE
19 21
Route
10
Oxford Street
and
Kensington
High Street
10
Euston Oxford Street
Marble Arch
Knightsbridge
HAMMERSMITH BDY.
TURKEY
A Paradise Preserved.
Kensington
Knightsbridge
Oxford Street
King's Cross
RM 2136
LONDON NORTHERN
CUV136C

London Central is the LBL subsidiary with the largest Routemaster allocation, and their route 36 has the largest service requirement at 46 vehicles on Mondays to Fridays. Showbus RM 9 looks exceptionally well looked after in this May 1992 view at Lewisham. Stephen Madden

RMs allocated to training work have declined in number since new legislation was introduced in 1991. RM23, in the hands of a new driver at Queen Elizabeth Road, Kingston in June 1992, shows the extended radiator which has been fitted to many of the survivors to enable them to meet the new rules. Geoff Rixon

One of the first RMLs to be refurbished was also one of the oldest. Brixton's RML895, fitted with an Iveco engine, rounds Marble Arch in August 1992, and may well achieve its 40th birthday in service if the lifespan expected for these vehicles is fulfilled. Tony Wilson

RML2456 represents the refurbished RML with Cummins engine. It was one of those retrieved from London Country towards the end of the 1970s and was seen at Mansion House in July 1992. East London is the only LBL subsidiary with a mixture of engine types within its RML fleet. Stephen Madden

Victoria's RML2516 was fitted with platform doors and given cream relief in October 1991, unofficially becoming DRM2516 in the process. In the first view it passes Hyde Park Corner on route 19 in September 1992, in the days before the route became the first crewed service to be offered for tender, being transferred to Kentish Bus in April 1993. Stephen Madden

In this rear view of 'DRM2516' the doorway arrangement can be clearly seen. During summer 1992 a special service was worked from central London to the Dulwich Picture Gallery, using the vehicle, and here it is displaying suitable notices. It has since been refurbished, somewhat contrary to expectations. Stephen Madden

Two RMAs remain available for passenger service with East London, and can usually be found on route 15 on most weekdays. Here, however, RMA8 cuts a handsome figure when on loan to London United in connection with their open day at Hounslow garage on 12th September 1992. Tony Wilson

Seven RMCs still appear in passenger service with East London. Officially now allocated to Leyton, Upton Park and North Street for training duties, in practice three or four per day are used as back-ups on route 15. On 18th May 1992 RMC1461 turns into Regent Street when the 15 service ran through to Ladbroke Grove. Capital Transport

Just six Fleetlines remain for use by passengers, and all are used only on special services. D2600, a B20 version, was one of the last examples which could be sampled in regular service when used on school routes 345 and 449 from North Street garage. Tony Wilson

Open-top DMS2291, bodied by MCW, has continued to be used on summer services, as well as appearing on private hire work and other special occasions. It can be found on fine days on summer route 333 through the Lee Valley Park, but here on a less than fine day in 1992 it was found passenger-less on route 73. Russell Upcraft

Almost all of the surviving B20 trainers are with London General, who have painted them in this striking livery and given them unofficial DMT classifications. Park Royal-bodied DMT2476 was photographed in May 1992 well outside its normal territory at Brighton on the day of the HCVS London to Brighton Rally. Tony Wilson

The five prototype Metrobuses, distinguished by their three-piece front destination blinds, are now usually confined to driver training work. However, along with a few Titans, they double as 'special duty' vehicles and M3 was found on 3rd April 1993 on rail replacement work at Bridge Street, Pinner. Colin Lloyd

At school times, certain journeys on route H12 are in the hands of Metrobuses, even though the main all-day service is with Darts. Here Harrow Weald's M937, with unrepaired front dome damage, passes one of the several schools on the route, in Headstone Lane. Tony Wilson

M1429, bedecked with Metroline Travel logos, is one of several similarly attired vehicles at Metroline's garages for use on private hire work. Here it is seen at Marble Arch on the Sunday opo version of route 98, which replaced the western end of route 8 in the big Central London route re-shuffle of July 1992. Tony Wilson

Leaside Buses have a very large fleet of Metrobuses, most of them standard machines. M1214, at Wood Green Station, is one of these, except that the front upper-deck windows have been modified to be non-opening, common nowadays on Titans but quite rare on Metrobuses. Mike Harris

The Airbus services between Central London and Heathrow Airport are in the hands of coach-seated Metrobuses. In the past year they have been given an attractive new livery and colour-coded blinds as shown in these nearside and offside views at Hyde Park Corner and Russell Square. Stephen Madden/John Miller

M1069 has continued to operate in London United 'tramway' livery from Fulwell garage, and carries the full-colour version of the London United coat-of-arms. This shot of the vehicle leaving the Hammersmith Grove terminus of route 267 shows the clean lines of the livery to striking effect. Tony Wilson

The two MkII Metrobuses accompanied the Cummins-engined MkI examples to Croydon garage in March 1992. Route 109 remains one of their haunts after the transfer from Streatham. M1442 is seen at Westminster. Stephen Madden

Low-bridge accidents continue to provide a steady flow of open-toppers to the fleet! One of the latest is M804, neatly converted for use on summer route Z1 between Baker Street and the London Zoo. Although now minus its central exit door, the running number position has stayed amidships. Tony Wilson

The five ex-Greater Manchester single-door Metrobuses were transferred from Wood Green to Enfield in June 1992 and are officially intended solely for route 317, although they also appear at times on other services. M1447, showing evidence of a hastily-fitted blind, cruises through Waltham Cross on 20th June 1992. Colin Lloyd

The two Alexander-bodied Metrobuses acquired from Yorkshire Rider have remained at Potters Bar. Here M1449 stands at Hertford bus station, the northernmost point reached by regular LBL services and the terminus of route 310A, a rare example of an LBL commercial competitive service, in being since D-Day in October 1986. Colin Lloyd

A reprieve from sale has been gained by T80, which was converted to single-door format in June 1992. This view at Woodford Wells three months later seems to give the vehicle a longer appearance than its dual-door colleagues. In contrast to M804 two pages back, the running number position has been moved forward. Tony Wilson

Found at Whipps Cross in October 1992, T258 is one of the 13 Titans which were completed at Workington from parts provided by Park Royal when production was transferred. Gold relief and gold fleetnames are carried by T258, like several East London Titans, a legacy of earlier use on Docklands services. Tony Wilson

Actually still based at Barking in spite of the CH garage code, T470 represents the standard traditional opening front upper-deck window Titan. It is in Ilford on route 128, one of several new or altered routes in the large route change scheme of 20th March 1993 in the Ilford-Barking area. Mike Harris

T1000 was one of the earlier examples of newer vehicles acquiring registrations from Routemasters, in this case from RM2001. It had been fitted with a dot-matrix destination screen when tracked down on route 35 at the Elephant & Castle on New Year's Day 1993. Mike Harris

Westlink holds a batch of Titans for use on LT tendered route 131, though the original examples are now being replaced by overhauled machines. T911 is seen at East Molesey in March 1993. Geoff Rixon

The five Titans acquired from West Midlands remain in use for private hire and occasional express service at Plumstead, New Cross and North Street. New Cross based T1129 shows its London Central Travel livery to good effect in this view at Ludgate Circus on 15th June 1992. Stephen Madden

T512, converted to open-top in 1988 after a low bridge accident, is often seen on local bus routes in East London, usually with the upper deck sealed off. However on 12th September 1992 it was loaned to London United for use on a special circular service H99 from Hounslow which circumnavigated Heathrow Airport. Colin Lloyd

Leaside Buses, having briefly flirted with Titans in 1991/92, lost them again. However more recently some have come back into their stock for training or private hire work. Several of the trainers, now based at Clapton, have acquired the unofficial 'TT' class letters, and TT58 is seen at Southgate. Stephen Madden

The three evaluatory Olympians with Eastern Coach Works bodies continue in use at Croydon. L1 was caught near the end of its trip into Croydon from the sprawling New Addington estates.
Colin Lloyd

Thornton Heath is responsible for operating more than 60 Olympians on six LT tendered routes. L27, having gained a former Routemaster registration in 1991, leaves Old Town, Clapham Common for Croydon on route 60.
Tony Wilson

An Olympian in red and gold London Central Travel livery, even though retaining bus rather than coach-type seating, is L96. It was found at Elephant & Castle on ordinary bus work in January 1993.
Stephen Madden

L167 is one of six Olympians allocated to Norwood garage with coach type seating for use on express service X68. It is seen at Russell Square. Stephen Madden

L136 has continued to operate in LT Tramways livery to mark the centenary of tramways in Lewisham. Seen at Greenwich in April 1992, it shows the non-reflective number plate and the gold fleet number (without the L prefix) which harmonise with the attractive livery. Some Selkent Routemasters have also received this style of registration plate. Tony Wilson

The 23 Olympians based at Stamford Brook carry Riverside Bus motifs and are primarily intended for daily use on LT route 237, although they can also also be found on route 27, and now work the 9 on weekday evenings and the 94 on weekday evenings and Sundays. L301 is seen in Regent Street in March 1993. Mike Harris

Leaside Buses received 40 Olympians with Alexander bodywork during the first half of 1992, placing them all at Stamford Hill garage to replace a temporary allocation of Titans. L316 is seen at Stamford Hill on the frequent 253 service, a route with a Monday to Friday requirement of 46 buses. Stephen Madden

Interior view of the upper deck of one of the Stamford Hill Olympians, L353. The new style seating moquette is now being adopted as standard by London Buses following its successful use on the refurbished RMLs. Adrian Clifford

The Volvo Ailsas with Alexander bodywork are now reduced to two. V2 passes through Enfield on 27th March 1993; note that the upper-deck front windows no longer match. Both are now officially relegated to spares, though regularly appearing on route W8. Colin Lloyd

The Volvo Citybus fleet has expanded to 39 vehicles, all based at Stockwell and chiefly used on LT routes 133 and 196, though also appearing at times on the 37, 49, 77A and 337. VC1 is one of 15 to so far have taken registrations from Routemasters, and here pauses at Streatham Hill in March 1993. Mike Harris

The original nine Scanias with Alexander bodywork have remained based at Potters Bar for LT route 263, and were all given their first repaint during 1992. S1 rounds Tally-Ho Corner at North Finchley in August 1992. Tony Wilson

The closing months of 1991 saw the arrival of 20 further Scania/Alexanders with East London. In the summer of 1992 nine were moved to Holloway and treated to this striking livery for Red Express X43, on which S17 is seen in Holloway Road in August 1992. It is surprising that such new vehicles should earn their keep on just two return trips a day. Tony Wilson

During 1992 a further 40 Scanias arrived with East London, this time bodied by Northern Counties and with dual doorway bodywork. S35 is one of a total of 20 Scanias in Docklands Express livery, and was appropriately caught amid Docklands reconstruction. Tony Wilson

The other half of East London's Northern Counties Scanias are in standard bus livery and allocated for routes 15B and 26, though they also appear on other routes worked by their two garages at Upton Park and Bow. S50 is seen at Mansion House. Stephen Madden

Delivery of 25 DAF/Optare Spectras was completed early in the New Year of 1993. The last of the batch, SP25, shows the striking lines of this design well as it turns right at Oxford Circus on 20th March 1993 on route 3, the principal daily operation for the type. Colin Lloyd

The second Spectra was built to dual-door design for evaluation by Metroline, in which guise it was seen at Cricklewood on 3rd November 1992. However within a few months SP2 was moved to join its single-doored sisters at Camberwell. Tony Wilson

The rear of the Spectra body, which unusually lacks a rear lower-deck window, naturally lends itself to advertising and several SPs have been given this treatment. SP15 shows the application as it crosses Lambeth Bridge. Stephen Madden

Upper deck interior view of an SP, showing the individual seating fitted. Capital Transport

RV1, an AEC Regent V/Park Royal originally with East Kent, was purchased by Leaside in 1991, and evokes interesting speculation as to what might have been had Routemasters not seen the light of day. Allocated to Stamford Hill for private hire, training duties and school work, it was found at Waltham Cross advertising private hire, and at Stamford Hill returning from a training session. Tony Wilson/Stephen Madden

Such BLs as remained proved ideal for the training fleet under new legislation from 1991 and were eagerly seized upon by CentreWest and London United, though the latter is now replacing them with Routemasters. BL1, part of the CentreWest contingent, shows the attention which has been paid to the conversion of the type. Stephen Madden

It is necessary to visit Westlink territory to see MkI Leyland Nationals in normal service. LS30 was one of six converted to single-door dual-purpose configuration in 1986, and is seen at Hampton Court on Surrey County Council route 592, its regular duty. Geoff Rixon

The Mk2 Leyland Nationals were originally all used for Red Arrow services and most still are. The latest livery with the large fleetname and roundel at roof level is shown by LS448 at the roundabout off Lambeth Bridge. Stephen Madden

Ten of the Mk2 Leyland Nationals have been converted to single-door and fitted with high-back seating for use on the 607 Express service from Uxbridge. LS503, its registration commandeered from a redundant RMC, enters Shepherds Bush Green on 2nd May 1992. Colin Lloyd

Above **Though some have been leased by LT to other contract operators, six LSs remain with London Buses for Mobility Bus services from North Street and Peckham garages. LS105, numerically the oldest of these and the only one converted for its new purpose by PMT, approaches Whipps Cross in October 1992.** Tony Wilson

Left **The conversion of the centre exit door on the Mobility Bus Leyland Nationals into a wheelchair lift is shown in this view of the nearside of LS156. This particular vehicle is now sold, its route having been transferred to another operator in 1992.** Capital Transport

Facing Page **LS466 was sent for Greenway conversion and returned in October 1992 in rebuilt form, being renumbered GLS1, and returned for Red Arrow service with London General. The cleaner lines are evident in these views. A further 41 Greenway conversions are now under way for the Red Arrow fleet.** Stephen Madden

507
VICTORIA STATION
Lambeth Bridge
WATERLOO STATION
RED ARROW
LONDON GENERAL
RED ARROW
GUW 466W

RED ARROW
507
LONDON GENERAL
GUW 466W

CentreWest also obtained a Greenway, converted from a former North Western/Crosville machine and initially operated in London under its former registration of FCA9X. GLS2 runs alongside Nationals and Lynxes on the 607 Express from Uxbridge, being seen at Hayes End. David Barrow

The first two Leyland Lynxes in the London Buses fleet arrived at the end of 1988 for use at Uxbridge on local route 128 and were in a special livery for that purpose. When the route ceased, they stayed at Uxbridge but have now been treated to 607 Express livery. LX2 enters Uxbridge bus station on 16th April 1992. Colin Lloyd

Six LSs went to Shepherds Bush for the 283 route in September 1988, moving to Stamford Brook four months later, and were transferred to route 190 when the 283 was converted to Dart. LX7, with the yellow blinds characteristic of Riverside Bus operations, stands at Chiswick in August 1991. Tony Wilson

All nine of the earlier DAF/Optare Deltas are now based with Westlink, and eight of them (DAs 2-9) are used on route 110. DA1 is in a special livery, inherited from its days with East London, for private hire work. DA3 shows the standard Westlink livery to good effect in this view at Hounslow. Russell Upcraft

The 26 Deltas allocated to East London carry this silver and red livery style. DA18 passes through Barking on 20th March 1993, working a new route introduced that day as part of an area scheme to replace parts of the 169, B1 and B2. Russell Upcraft

The rear styling of the Delta is depicted in this view in Ilford, taken before the 20th March changes as the 129 no longer has Deltas and the 247 no longer runs to Ilford. Note the 'green' sticker in the rear window to imply a more environmentally friendly bus. Stephen Madden

Selkent purchased the first 16 Dennis Lances in LBL use during 1992, specifying bodywork by Alexander and taking the opportunity to introduce a revised livery. LA11, with an out-of-sequence registration, passes along Downham Way on 13th June 1992. R.J. Waterhouse

The LAs have a neat rear elevation, and this view of LA3 emphasises the length of the type. Single deckers have been allocated to the busy 36B service because of problems with vandalism in some of the areas it serves when double deckers were used. Stephen Madden

Metroline ordered 31 Dennis Lances for routes 113 and 302, but unlike Selkent's these were fitted with the new Northern Counties Paladin body. The company would not put them into service until all drivers were trained, the first allocation being to Willesden for the 302 on 24th April 1993. LN29 is seen at Neasden. Tony Wilson

Opposite **Similar bodywork to the Lances is mounted onto Volvo B10B chassis as the VN class for London General's route 88. The class entered service on 15th May 1993 and is marketed as the Clapham Omnibus, recalling the famous 'Man on the Clapham Omnibus' tag coined by a judge in 1903. VNs 8 and 9 are seen at Oxford Circus.** Tony Wilson

HENNES
HENNES
CLAPHAM COMMON
88
VN 8
Clapham
OMNIBUS
LONDON BUSES
VOLVO
Clapham
OMNIBUS
K8 KLL

88
K9
KLL
Clapham
OMNIBUS
Clapham
OMNIBUS
73

Westlink have increased their holding of Omnis to six. Here CV2, from the original batch intended for route H20, strays onto route R62 at Twickenham RFU Ground on 16th May 1992. Note the height of the driving position compared with the passenger seating. Mike Harris

DRs provided the midibus element of the Wandsworth scheme introduced in May 1991. Merton's DR37 stands in Wimbledon bus station on 5th September 1992, and shows the 'Streetline' marketing name applied to most of its midibus operations by London General. Mike Harris

In London United's territory, DRs are marketed under the 'Harrier' name. The Wood Lane outstation has a 100% DR allocation and on 27th March 1993 took over the Sunday service on route 220, to allow Shepherds Bush garage to be closed henceforth on that day of the week. DR125 pauses at Hammersmith, Butterwick. J.G.S. Smith

The DR also exists in stretched form. The first 16 DRLs are based at Peckham, whence DRL 4 was seen in August 1992. The first four have been named after characters in the Only Fools and Horses TV series, DRL 4 being Uncle Albert. Tony Wilson

The DT class had bodywork by Duple or Carlyle, the majority being the latter. DT84 is one of these and is seen in Hampton Court Road on 8th September 1991 on route R68, a service which replaced the section of the old 267 south of Fulwell Garage. Mike Harris

Selkent's DT32, with the 'Roundabout' fleetnames which are a legacy from the original minibus scheme in Orpington when a maroon livery was used, is seen in its home town. It carries a former RM registration and has been rebuilt with a larger blind box as fitted to similar vehicles with Luton & District. Tony Wilson

The largest single variant of the Dart has been the DW, bodied by Wright Brothers in Ballymena, Northern Ireland, and all but a handful carry a marketing name. London General's 'Streetline' version on DW53 is seen here on route 355 at Clapham Common in March 1993. Mike Harris

The largest single allocation of DWs is at Westbourne Park with CentreWest, where they replaced the earlier MA class on the 'Gold Arrow' routes after they proved to be too small for the loads. DW 77 illustrates the use of the vehicles on Sundays on route 7. Tony Wilson

The most recent DWs were 38 used in the Barking/Ilford scheme on 20th March 1993, together with 12 of the stretched version, classified DWL, for route 62. DWL 25 is seen in Barking. Colin Lloyd

The DWL was first introduced with 14 allocated to Westlink at Kingston in December 1990 for LT route 371. However DWL1, seen here in June 1992, is in a special livery and is habitually used on contract work for Kingston University (the institution having recently been upgraded from Polytechnic status). Stephen Madden

The first FMs entered service in late April 1993, somewhat later than anticipated. They reintroduced Marshall bodywork to the London Buses fleet after many years, the last being the SM class of AEC Swifts in the early 1970s. They have replaced most of the RHs on Orpington's Roundabout network. FM10 is seen in the town centre. Tony Wilson

Eight Ivecos with Reeve Burgess conversions suitable for wheelchair passengers are based at Hounslow for routes H24 and H25, supported by the London Borough of Hounslow, and carrying a small amount of the lime green colour of the Borough's vehicles. FR8 shows the livery style at Hanworth, Butts Farm on 12th January 1991. Mike Harris

The FS class of Ford Transits is reduced to just one survivor. Westlink's FS29, converted by Carlyle Works, makes a rare catch for the photographer in Hounslow High Street as it performs staff bus duties. Mike Harris

Five Mercedes with Carlyle Works bodywork, including an ex-demonstrator, reside at Orpington. MC5, the last of the batch, leaves the town's shopping area as the photographer stands by the War Memorial landmark. Route R3 is their normal allocation. Stephen Madden

The initial batch of 107 Mercedes-Benz with Alexander bodywork all went to CentreWest, though some have since been passed to Selkent. Over one third were deployed to Uxbridge under the U Line marketing banner. However in spring 1993 these names were painted out and a new Uxbridge Buses logo began to be applied, MA81 being one of the first two. It is seen in April 1993 on the Sunday-only U8 route, due for withdrawal in June. Tony Wilson

Two further batches of MAs, totalling 27, were ordered by London General for 'Streetline' operations on routes 39, 239 and 265 from Victoria Basement and Putney garages. MA114 awaits departure from Putney Bridge Station on 26th August 1991. Mike Harris

Early batches of Metroriders are now being withdrawn, although several are allocated as spare vehicles around the fleet, and have been used to inaugurate new services such as the 303 at Edgware. MR7, one of the initial batch delivered to Westlink, was still going strong at Kingston on 5th September 1992.
Colin Lloyd

Six MRs have 'Wandsworth Health Authority' logos, initially because of their exclusive use on routes G1 and G2 which served several hospitals in the area. Subsequent route and allocation changes have meant that they are used on any of Norwood's minibus routes, as here with MR96 on the Sunday operation of route 118.
Russell Upcraft

Leaside Buses have held on to three MRs at Clapton garage, used exclusively on a contract service 'The Shuttle' for the DHSS, ferrying staff between hospitals and health centres in Central and inner West London. MR105 is crossing Westminster Bridge.
Stephen Madden

The East London Hoppa minibus routes worked by West Ham and Bow garages all moved to a new base near Stratford on 26th September 1992 and eventually the WH and BW codes gave way to SD. WH's MRLs and BW's RBs are now all mixed. John Miller

More recent Metroriders have been built by Optare at Leeds to fast-flow door specification. Merton's MRL183 is a typical example, but within London General is fairly unusual in being a 'Hoppa' rather than a 'Streetline'! Stephen Madden

More Mercedes, this time with Reeve Burgess bodies fitted with tail-lifts for wheelchair access, can be found with CentreWest. MT3 is one of five in Southall Shuttle livery for use on route E5 between Greenford (its base) and Southall. However here it is helping out on Mobility Bus route 976 and has just arrived in Hounslow. Stephen Madden

One of the MTs (MT6) was delivered in stretched form and was subsequently transferred to the more appropriate MTL class, as MTL6. It carries high-back seats and performs as a private hire vehicle with Selkent, also doubling as a training bus. With its ex-Routemaster registration, it speeds through Charlton on 10th April 1992. Tony Wilson

Sixteen further Mercedes were bodied by Wright Brothers in 1989 and introduced Irish registrations to the capital. All the first sixteen work at Catford garage, as demonstrated by MW3 at Rushey Green, Catford in May 1992 on the Sunday operation of route 75. Twenty others entered service in May 1993 at Potters Bar with London Northern. Russell Upcraft

A one-off is MW17 which, although essentially similar to other MWs, looks radically different due to its modified front-end styling. After a stint at Victoria Basement it moved early in 1993 to Uxbridge where it is unique among hordes of MAs. It is seen departing from Uxbridge Bus Station. Tony Wilson

Renaults made a rather surprising appearance on the London scene in 1990. RB6, one of an initial batch of 25 with Reeve Burgess bodies ordered for East London, waits time at Morning Lane, Hackney on 25th April 1992. All of the type now works alongside MRLs from the new outstation at Stratford. Mike Harris

The oldest minibuses still in regular use, the RH class of Ivecos with Robin Hood conversions, is now reduced to four, nominally as spare buses following the commissioning of the new FM class. All are at Orpington, their home since new. RH5, one of the four survivors, pauses in Orpington High Street. John G.S. Smith

Wright bodied a further 90 Renaults for CentreWest's Ealing area scheme in 1990. Though most carry 'E-Line' branding, a few carry 'hoppa' names with CentreWest's gold arrow logo and are used on route 282, as demonstrated by RW5 at Northwood Hills on 20th August 1991. Since March 1993 the entire class works from the new base at Greenford. Tony Wilson

The Optare StarRider was introduced to London in 1988 and achieved a total of 123 vehicles in just over eighteen months. SR12, now moved to Norwood to cope with new route 322, stands at Crystal Palace on 30th March 1993. The 'Connexions' branding, first just for the 322, has now been applied to most other midibuses at Norwood. Colin Lloyd

Perhaps the most remarkable vehicle in the London Buses coaching fleets is SKY1, a Neoplan Skyliner purchased in 1991 by London Northern. Here it poses outside the Tufnell Park end of Holloway garage in April 1992. Much of its time is spent touring abroad, and it is a comparatively rare sight within London. Tony Wilson

Selkent Travel is a thriving private hire operation with eight coaches in stock. This Van Hool bodied DAF has been given a new livery and was photographed at the Brighton Coach Rally. Selkent

Leaside Buses have five coaches in their private hire fleet, of which LPs 5 and 6 came from Cambus of Cambridge. Although bound for the exhibition centre at Olympia, it is seen on home territory in Alexandra Park. Tony Wilson

East London Coaches operate three Plaxton bodied Leyland Tiger coaches on their private hire and excursion work. Although delivered in dealer white they have been treated to this striking red striping. TPL7 is at home base, North Street Romford (note the garage code on the driver's window). Tony Wilson

1992 saw Metroline Travel branch into the coach field. LD5, seen at Edgware in October 1992, has Duple coachwork of a design more familiar on Scottish coaches, on its Leyland Leopard chassis, and was acquired from Beeston of Hadleigh in Suffolk, with whom it had begun life in 1982. Tony Wilson

Some of the most recent additions to the coach fleet came to Metroline in time for the 1993 season. Two Duple 320-bodied Tigers form the TDL class, and TDL2 poses at North Wembley. It retains the cream-based livery of Shearings, its previous owners, adapted to good effect by the new operator. Tony Wilson

FLEET LISTS

DOUBLE DECKERS

Listed in the order: RT/RM/RML/RMC/RMA/RV/DMS/D/DM/M/T/L/V/VC/S/SP

RT

Chassis AEC Regent III 0961
Engine AEC A204 9.6-litre rated at 89kW at 1800 rpm
Bodywork Weymann H30/26R
Built 1949
Dimensions 7918mm x 2286mm x 4351mm
Number Built 4825
Number in Stock 1

1530w KGU290

w Withdrawn

RM/RML/RMC

RM 5-872, RML 880-903, RM 906-1435, RMC 1453-1515, RM 1527-2217, RML 2261-2760

Sub frames AEC Routemaster R2RH (RM 2099: 2R2RH, RML 2261-2760: R2RH/1)
Engine Cummins 6CT8.3 8.27-litre rated at 112kW at 2200rpm (a: AEC AV590 9.6-litre rated at 86kW at 1800rpm, i: Iveco 8361 8.1-litre rated at 97kW at 1800rpm, y: Leyland 0600 9.8-litre rated at 86kW at 1800rpm)
Bodywork Park Royal H36/28R (RMs, except RM 644 is O36/28R), H32/25RD (RMCs, except RMC 1464 is O36/25RD, RMC1490 is H25/22RD and RMC 1510/5 are O32/25RD), H40/32R (RMLs, except RML 2516 is H40/32RD)
Built 1958-1968
Dimensions 8395mm x 2426mm x 4382mm (RM/RMC), 9106mm x 2426mm x 4382mm (RML)
Number Built 2760
Number in Stock 754 (262 RM, 478 RML, 14 RMC)
Number Scheduled for Service 521 (86 RM, 435 RML)

RM

5a VLT5
***6** VLT6
9a OYM374A
***13**aw KGJ83A
***14**a OYM424A
18i VLT18
23at VLT23
25at VLT25
29a OYM453A
32a VLT32
***46**i OYM580A
53i OYM582A
70at VLT70
***71**at VLT71
***89**gi VLT89
***98**aw KGJ28A
180au XVS830
202a VLT202
244a XVS839
264au VLT264
268a VLT268
***275**a VLT275
295a VLT295
311i KGJ142A
317au WLT317
324a WLT324
329at WLT329
339at WLT339
342a WLT342
346i SVS615
348i WLT348
379aw GVS479
385at WLT385
395i WLT395
***402**au WLT402
423a WLT423
432i SVS617
436a WLT436
446a WLT446
463a KGH899A
467i WLT467
470i WLT470
474i GVS480
478a WLT478
487au XVS827
516a WLT516
522aw WLT522
527a WLT527
531i WLT531
541a WLT541
548i SVS618
554aw KGH883A
***598**i WLT598
599i WLT599
613a WLT613
***625**a WLT625
644ao WLT644
646a WLT646
648au XVS826
659a WLT659
664i WLT664
676i WLT676
687a WLT687
688a WLT688
696au XVS829
***701**au WLT701
719a WLT719
735a WLT735
***736**a WLT736
758a WLT758
765a WLT765
782a WLT782
787a WLT787
***789**a WLT789
***801**aw WLT801
803aw KGJ24A
***804**at WLT804
***815**a WLT815
826a WLT826
837au KGJ62A
838at WLT838
843au XVS828
868a WLT868
***872**a WLT872

RML

880f WLT880
†881 WLT881
†882 WLT882
†883 WLT883
†884 WLT884
†885 WLT885
†886 WLT886
†887i WLT887
†888 WLT888
†889i WLT889
†890 WLT890
†891 WLT891
†892i WLT892
893 WLT893
†894i WLT894
†895i WLT895
896 WLT896
897 WLT897
898i WLT898
†899i WLT899
†901 WLT901
†902 WLT902
903a WLT903

RM

906aw WLT906
912a WLT912
***916**aw GVS491
920at WLT920
928a WLT928
931at WLT931
940a WLT940
944a WLT944
946at WLT946
966au WLT966
967a WLT967
970i WLT970
977au WLT977
***990**at WLT990
†994i WLT994
995a WLT995
997i WLT997
1002a OYM368A
1003i 3CLT
***1005**a ALC290A
1018au PVS828
1019au PVS829
1020au PVS830
1023aw KGH956A
1033a 33CLT
1046aw EGF282B
1058a 58CLT
1062a 62CLT
1070a 70CLT
1078a KGH925A
1081a 81CLT
1082a 82CLT
1083i 83CLT
1089a ALC179A
1097a 97CLT
1101i KGH969A
1102au 102CLT
1104a 104CLT
1119a 119CLT
1124a 124CLT
1125i KGH858A
1133a 133CLT
1138a 138CLT
1141au 141CLT
1158a 158CLT
1162aw 162CLT
1168a 168CLT
1170at 170CLT
1171a 171CLT
1174a 174CLT
1175a 175CLT
1185a 185CLT
1186i 186CLT
1197aw KGJ29A
1204a 204CLT
1205a 205CLT
1209au 209CLT
1214a 214CLT
1217aw KGH887A
1218a 218CLT

1219i	219CLT
1236at	236CLT
1240a	240CLT
1257at	257CLT
1260a	260CLT
1266au	266CLT
1277au	277CLT
1283a	283CLT
1287a	287CLT
1292a	NVS485
1304i	304CLT
1305a	305CLT
1312i	312CLT
1324a	324CLT
1327aw	327CLT
1330a	KGH975A
1348a	348CLT
1350aw	350CLT
1352i	SVS616
1361a	361CLT
1380a	380CLT
1392aw	392CLT
1398a	398CLT
1400a	400CLT
1428au	428CLT
1435a	KGJ184A

RMC

1453au	453CLT
1456ab	456CLT
1458ab	458CLT
1461ab	461CLT
1464io	464CLT
1469at	469CLT
1485ab	485CLT
1486aw	KVS276
1490ab	490CLT
1492at	492CLT
1496ab	496CLT
1510ao	510CLT
1513ab	513CLT
1515ao	515CLT

RM

1527at	527CLT
1528i	528CLT
1545au	KGJ37A
1562a	562CLT
1568a	568CLT
1585a	585CLT
1590gi	590CLT
1593i	593CLT
1609a	609DYE
1619au	KGJ188A
1621au	KGJ187A
1656aw	KGH932A
1666a	666DYE
1676a	676DYE
1681at	681DYE
1698aw	KGJ173A
1700a	KGJ167A
1725at	725DYE
1727a	727DYE
1734i	734DYE
1750aw	750DYE
1758a	758DYE
1770a	770DYE
1772a	772DYE
1782at	782DYE
1797a	797DYE
1799a	799DYE
1801i	801DYE
1804a	804DYE
1809aw	EBY257B
1811i	EGF220B
1815aw	EGF286B
1822i	822DYE
1825au	825DYE
1832a	832DYE
1836au	EGF285B
1840a	840DYE
1872i	ALD872B
1882au	ALD882B
1894i	ALD894B
1946a	ALD946B
1948a	ALD948B
1955a	ALD955B
1962a	ALD962B
1970aw	ALD970B
1971a	ALD971B
1977a	ALD977B
1978i	ALD978B
1979a	ALD979B
1980a	ALD980B
1992a	ALD992B
2000a	ALM200B
2002at	ALM2B
2003at	ALM3B
2008a	ALM8B
2021a	ALM21B
2022a	ALM22B
2023a	ALM23B
2033	ALM33B
2041a	ALM41B
2046a	ALM46B
2050a	ALM50B
2051a	ALM51B
2078au	ALM78B
2079au	ALM79B
2082a	ALM82B
2090a	ALM90B
2097a	ALM97B
2099uy	ALM99B
2103au	ALM103B
2104aw	ALM104B
2106a	CUV106C
2109a	CUV109C
2112at	CUV112C
2128a	CUV128C
2129a	CUV129C
2131au	CUV131C
2132au	CUV132C
2136a	CUV136C
2151a	CUV151C
2153a	CUV153C
2173a	CUV173C
2179i	CUV179C
2181au	CUV181C
2183a	CUV183C
2186a	CUV186C
2187a	CUV187C
2201at	CUV201C
2204aw	CUV204C
2209au	CUV209C
2213a	CUV213C
2217i	CUV217C

RML

†**2261**	CUV261C
†**2262**i	CUV262C
†**2263**i	CUV263C
†**2264**i	CUV264C
2265	CUV265C
†**2267**	CUV267C
2268	CUV268C
†**2269**	CUV269C
2270	CUV270C
2271	CUV271C
2272	CUV272C
2273	CUV273C
2274	CUV274C
* †**2275**	CUV275C
†**2276**	CUV276C
2277	CUV277C
2278	CUV278C
2279	CUV279C
2280	CUV280C
2281	CUV281C
†**2282**	CUV282C
2283	CUV283C
†**2284**	CUV284C
2285	CUV285C
†**2286**	CUV286C
†**2287**	CUV287C
2288	CUV288C
2289	CUV289C
2290i	CUV290C
†**2291**	CUV291C
†**2292**	CUV292C
†**2293**	CUV293C
†**2294**	CUV294C
†**2295**	CUV295C
†**2296**	CUV296C
†**2297**i	CUV297C
†**2298**	CUV298C
2299	CUV299C
2300i	CUV300C
2302	CUV302C
2303i	CUV303C
†**2304**	CUV304C
2305i	CUV305C
2307i	CUV307C
2308	CUV308C
2309	CUV309C
†**2310**	CUV310C
†**2311**	CUV311C
2312	CUV312C
2313	CUV313C
2314	CUV314C
2315	CUV315C
†**2316**i	CUV316C
†**2317**i	CUV317C
2318	CUV318C
†**2321**i	CUV321C
2322	CUV322C
2323	CUV323C
†**2324**i	CUV324C
†**2325**	CUV325C
†**2326**	CUV326C
2327	CUV327C
†**2328**	CUV328C
†**2329**	CUV329C
2330	CUV330C
2331	CUV331C
†**2332**	CUV332C
†**2333**i	CUV333C
2334	CUV334C
2335	CUV335C
†**2336**	CUV336C
2338	CUV338C
2339	CUV339C
2340	CUV340C
2341	CUV341C
†**2342**i	CUV342C
†**2344**	CUV344C
2345	CUV345C
†**2346**	CUV346C
2348	CUV348C
†**2349**	CUV349C
†**2350**	CUV350C
2351i	CUV351C
†**2352**	CUV352C
†**2353**	CUV353C
†**2354**	CUV354C
†**2355**	CUV355C
†**2356**	CUV356C
2357	CUV357C
†**2358**i	CUV358C
†**2359**	CUV359C
†**2360**i	CUV360C
†**2361**i	CUV361C
2362	CUV362C
†**2363**i	CUV363C
†**2364**i	JJD364D
2365	JJD365D
†**2366**i	JJD366D
†**2367**	JJD367D
2368	JJD368D
2369	JJD369D
†**2370**	JJD370D
†**2371**i	JJD371D
†**2372**	JJD372D
†**2373**	JJD373D
†**2374**	JJD374D
2375i	JJD375D
2376i	JJD376D
2377	JJD377D
2378	JJD378D
2379	JJD379D
†**2380**	JJD380D
2381	JJD381D
2384	JJD384D
†**2385**i	JJD385D
†**2386**	JJD386D
2388	JJD388D
2389i	JJD389D
2390	JJD390D
2391	JJD391D
2392i	JJD392D
2393	JJD393D
†**2394**	JJD394D
†**2395**	JJD395D
†**2396**	JJD396D
2397	JJD397D
†**2398**i	JJD398D
2399i	JJD399D
†**2400**	JJD400D
†**2401**	JJD401D
†**2402**i	JJD402D
†**2403**i	JJD403D
2404	JJD404D
2405	JJD405D
†**2406**	JJD406D
†**2407**i	JJD407D
2408	JJD408D
2409	JJD409D
†**2411**	JJD411D
†**2412**i	JJD412D
†**2413**	JJD413D
†**2414**	JJD414D
†**2415**i	JJD415D
†**2416**	JJD416D
†**2418**	JJD418D
†**2419**	JJD419D
†**2422**i	JJD422D
†**2428**	JJD428D
†**2429**i	JJD429D
2430	JJD430D
2431	JJD431D
†**2432**	JJD432D
†**2434**	JJD434D
2435i	JJD435D
2437i	JJD437D
2439	JJD439D
2440	JJD440D
†**2441**i	JJD441D
†**2442**	JJD442D
2443	JJD443D
2444i	JJD444D
†**2445**	JJD445D
2446	JJD446D
†**2447**	JJD447D
2450i	JJD450D
2451i	JJD451D
†**2453**i	JJD453D
2454	JJD454D
2455	JJD455D
†**2456**	JJD456D
†**2457**	JJD457D
†**2460**	JJD460D
†**2461**i	JJD461D
†**2462**i	JJD462D
†**2463**	JJD463D
†**2464**	JJD464D
†**2465**i	JJD465D
†**2466**i	JJD466D
2467	JJD467D
2468	JJD468D
2469	JJD469D
2470i	JJD470D
2471	JJD471D
†**2472**i	JJD472D
2473	JJD473D
2474	JJD474D
†**2475**i	JJD475D
2476	JJD476D
†**2477**i	JJD477D
2478	JJD478D
2479	JJD479D
2480	JJD480D
†**2481**i	JJD481D
2482	JJD482D
†**2483**	JJD483D
2484	JJD484D
†**2485**	JJD485D
2486	JJD486D
2487	JJD487D
†**2488**i	JJD488D
†**2489**	JJD489D
2490	JJD490D
†**2491**i	JJD491D
2492	JJD492D
2493i	JJD493D
2494	JJD494D
2495	JJD495D
†**2496**	JJD496D
†**2497**	JJD497D
†**2498**	JJD498D
2499	JJD499D
†**2500**	JJD500D
2501	JJD501D
†**2502**i	JJD502D
2503	JJD503D
2504	JJD504D
2506	JJD506D
2507	JJD507D
2508	JJD508D
†**2509**	JJD509D
2510	JJD510D
†**2511**	JJD511D
2513	JJD513D
2515	JJD515D
†**2516**di	JJD516D
†**2517**i	JJD517D
2518	JJD518D
2519	JJD519D
†**2520**i	JJD520D
†**2521**i	JJD521D
2522	JJD522D
2525	JJD525D
†**2526**	JJD526D
2527	JJD527D

†2528	JJD528D	**†2580**i	JJD580D	**2628**	NML628E	**2673**	SMK673F	**†2720**	SMK720F
†2529	JJD529D	**†2581**	JJD581D	**2629**	NML629E	**2674**	SMK674F	**†2721**	SMK721F
2530	JJD53D	**2582**	JJD582D	**2630**	NML630E	**†2675**	SMK675F	**†2722**	SMK722F
2532	JJD532D	**†2583**	JJD583D	**†2631**i	NML631E	**2676**	SMK676F	**†2723**	SMK723F
†2534	JJD534D	**2584**	JJD584D	**†2632**	NML632E	**†2677**	SMK677F	**2724**	SMK724F
†2535i	JJD535D	**2585**	JJD585D	**2633**	NML633E	**2678**	SMK678F	**†2725**i	SMK725F
2537i	JJD537D	**†2587**	JJD587D	**2634**	NML634E	**†2679**	SMK679F	**2726**i	SMK726F
2538i	JJD538D	**†2588**	JJD588D	**2635**	NML635E	**†2680**i	SMK680F	**†2727**	SMK727F
2539i	JJD539D	**2589**	JJD589D	**2636**i	NML636E	**2681**	SMK681F	**2728**	SMK728F
2540i	JJD540D	**†2590**	JJD590D	**2637**i	NML637E	**2682**	SMK682F	**†2729**	SMK729F
2541	JJD541D	**†2592**i	JJD592D	**2638**	NML638E	**†2683**	SMK683F	**†2730**i	SMK730F
†2542	JJD542D	**†2593**i	JJD593D	**†2639**	NML639E	**2684**	SMK684F	**†2731**	SMK731F
2543i	JJD543D	**2594**	JJD594D	**†2640**i	NML640E	**†2685**	SMK685F	**†2732**i	SMK732F
†2544	JJD544D	**†2595**	JJD595D	**†2641**	NML641E	**2686**	SMK686F	**†2733**	SMK733F
2545i	JJD545D	**2596**	JJD596D	**2642**	NML642E	**2687**	SMK687F	**†2734**	SMK734F
2546	JJD546D	**†2597**	JJD597D	**†2643**	NML643E	**†2688**	SMK688F	**2735**	SMK735F
2547	JJD547D	**2598**	JJD598D	**†2644**i	NML644E	**†2689**	SMK689F	**2736**i	SMK736F
†2549i	JJD549D	**2599**	NML599E	**†2645**	NML645E	**2690**	SMK690F	**2737**	SMK737F
†2550	JJD550D	**†2600**	NML600E	**†2646**	NML646E	**†2692**i	SMK692F	**2738**i	SMK738F
†2551	JJD551D	**2601**	NML601E	**2647**	NML647E	**†2693**i	SMK693F	**†2739**	SMK739F
†2552	JJD552D	**2602**	NML602E	**2648**i	NML648E	**2694**	SMK694F	**2740**	SMK740F
2553	JJD553D	**†2603**	NML603E	**2649**	NML649E	**2695**	SMK695F	**†2741**i	SMK741F
†2554	JJD554D	**2604**	NML604E	**†2650**	NML650E	**2696**at	SMK696F	**2742**	SMK742F
†2555	JJD555D	**†2605**i	NML605E	**2651**	NML651E	**†2697**	SMK697F	**2743**	SMK743F
2556	JJD556D	**†2606**i	NML606E	**2652**	NML652E	**2698**	SMK698F	**2744**	SMK744F
2558	JJD558D	**2607**i	NML607E	**2653**i	NML653E	**†2699**	SMK699F	**2745**i	SMK745F
2559	JJD559D	**†2608**i	NML608E	**†2654**i	NML654E	**2700**	SMK700F	**2746**	SMK746F
†2560	JJD560D	**2609**	NML609E	**2655**	NML655E	**†2701**	SMK701F	**2747**	SMK747F
†2561	JJD561D	**2610**	NML610E	**2656**	NML656E	**2702**	SMK702F	**2748**	SMK748F
2562	JJD562D	**†2611**	NML611E	**†2657**i	NML657E	**†2703**	SMK703F	**2749**i	SMK749F
2563	JJD563D	**†2612**i	NML612E	**†2658**	SMK658F	**†2704**	SMK704F	**2750**	SMK750F
†2564i	JJD564D	**†2613**	NML613E	**2659**	SMK659F	**†2705**	SMK705F	**†2751**	SMK751F
†2565	JJD565D	**2614**	NML614E	**2660**	SMK660F	**2706**	SMK706F	**†2752**i	SMK752F
2566	JJD566D	**†2615**i	NML615E	**†2661**	SMK661F	**†2707**	SMK707F	**†2753**i	SMK753F
†2567	JJD567D	**†2616**	NML616E	**2662**	SMK662F	**2708**	SMK708F	**2754**	SMK754F
†2568i	JJD568D	**2617**	NML617E	**2663**	SMK663F	**2709**i	SMK709F	**2755**	SMK755F
2569	JJD569D	**†2618**i	NML618E	**2664**	SMK664F	**†2710**	SMK710F	**2756**	SMK756F
2570i	JJD570D	**2620**	NML620E	**2665**i	SMK665F	**†2711**	SMK711F	**2757**	SMK757F
2571	JJD571D	**†2621**	NML621E	**2666**	SMK666F	**†2712**	SMK712F	**2758**at	SMK758F
†2572i	JJD572D	**†2622**	NML622E	**2667**	SMK667F	**†2713**	SMK713F	**2759**i	SMK759F
2573i	JJD573D	**2623**	NML623E	**2668**	SMK668F	**2714**	SMK714F	**2760**a	SMK760F
†2575i	JJD575D	**†2624**i	NML624E	**†2669**i	SMK669F	**2716**	SMK716F		
†2576i	JJD576D	**2625**	NML625E	**2670**	SMK670F	**2717**	SMK717F		
2578	JJD578D	**†2626**i	NML626E	**†2671**	SMK671F	**†2718**	SMK718F		
2579	JJD579D	**2627**	NML627E	**2672**	SMK672F	**2719**	SMK719F		

a AEC units b Beckton Express livery d Unofficially coded DRM 2516 f London United livery
g London General livery i Iveco units o Open top conversion t Trainer u Unlicensed w Withdrawn
y Leyland units * Fixed upper-deck front windows † Refurbished

Previous owners: RM 2050 re-acquired from Leaver, Sutton, 1989; RMC 1453-1515 and RML 2307-18/22-55/411-40/2/4-60 re-acquired from London Country, 1978 to 1980

Named vehicles: RMC 1456 *Prince Albert*, RMC 1458 *King George V*, RMC 1461 *Sir Christopher Wren*, RMC 1464 *Norwood Princess*, RMC 1485 *King William I*, RMC 1490 *King Edward VII*, RMC 1492 *Ruby*, RMC 1496 *Lord Nelson*, RMC 1513 *Queen Victoria*

RMA

Sub frames AEC Routemaster R2RH2
Engine AEC AV590 9.6-litre rated at 86kW at 1800rpm
Bodywork Park Royal H32/24F (RMA 5 is H32/25F)
Built 1967
Dimensions 8395mm x 2426mm x 4382mm
Number Built 65
Number in Stock 3

5	NMY635E	**8**	NMY640E	**55**t	NMY644E

t Trainer

Previous owner: RMA 8 acquired from LRT Bus Engineering Ltd, 1988

RV

Chassis AEC Regent V 2D3RA
Engine AEC AV590 9.6-litre rated at 86kW at 1800rpm
Bodywork Park Royal H40/32F
Built 1966
Dimensions 9144mm x 2426mm x 4420mm
Number in Stock 1

1	GJG750D	Acquired from Wealden PSV, Five Oak Green, 1991	Named *Harvey*

DMS/DM/D

DMS 681, DM 948-1102, DMS 1426-2499, D 2556, DM 2559, D 2600

Chassis Daimler CRL6-30 (681-1868) or Leyland FE30AGR (2168) or Leyland FE30ALR Special (2257-2600)
Engine Iveco 836-S 11-litre rated at 130kW at 2100rpm (g: Gardner 6LXB 10.45-litre rated at 127kW at 1850rpm, l: Leyland 0680 11.1-litre rated at 127kW at 1850rpm)
Bodywork Park Royal (681-1102, 2347-2600) or Metro-Cammell-Weymann (1426-2304)
Capacity H44/24D (681, 1426-1537, 1867-2290, 2304-2499), H44/27D (2559-2600), H44/31F (1657) O44/27D (948, 1102, 2556), O44/28D (2291)
Built 1970-1978
Dimensions 8398mm x 2502mm x 4420mm
Number Built 2646
Number in Stock 35 (2 D, 3 DM, 30 DMS)

681	MLK681L	**1867**lt	GHM867N	**2291**lo	THX291S	**2413**d	OJD413R	**2454**ltu	OJD454R
948lo	GHV948N	**1868**l	GHM868N	**2304**d	THX304S	**2425**w	OJD425R	**2476**d	THX476S
1102lo	GHV102N	**2168**g	OJD168R	**2347**d	OJD347R	**2432**w	OJD432R	**2489**d	THX489S
1426ltu	MLH426L	**2257**d	OJD257R	**2351**d	OJD351R	**2435**w	OJD435R	**2499**t	THX499S
1488ltu	MLH488L	**2281**d	THX281S	**2367**d	OJD367R	**2441**tu	OJD441R	**2559**w	THX559S
1537ltu	THM537M	**2283**d	THX283S	**2384**d	OJD384R	**2445**t	OJD445R	**2556**lo	THX556S
1657lz	THM657M	**2290**d	THX290S	**2397**d	OJD397R	**2453**ltu	OJD453R	**2600**l	THX600S

* Classified DM †Classified D
d Trainer, unofficially coded DMT g Gardner units l Leyland units o Open top conversion t Trainer u Unlicensed
w Withdrawn z On extended loan to Metropolitan Police College, Hendon (Bexleybus livery)

Previous owners: DMS 1657 ex Clydeside Scottish, 1987

Named vehicles: DM 948 *MV Royal Eagle*, DM 1102 *MV Royal Daffodil*, DMS 1867 *Gordon*

M

Sub-frames MCW Metrobus DR101/3 (M 1-5), DR101/4 (M 1481-1484), DR101/6 (M 1443-1447), DR101/8 (M 6-55), DR101/9 (M 56-205), DR101/12 (M 206-505), DR101/14 (M 506-805), DR101/15 (M 1448/9), DR101/16 (M 806-955), DR101/17 (M 956-1083, M 1106-1440), DR102/32 (M 1450/1), DR102/45 (M 1441), DR132/5 (M 1442), DR134/1 (M 1084-1105)

Engine Gardner 6LXB 10.45-litre rated at 127kW at 1850rpm (M 1084-1105, M 1442: Cummins LT10-B180 10-litre rated at 134kW at 1850rpm)

Bodywork Metro-Cammell-Weymann H43/28D+20 (M 19, 39, 43, 86, 96, 162 H43/9D+20; M 804 O43/30F+20; M 1006-29 H41/9DL+16; M 1080 H43/30F+20; M 1393/6 H37/27F+20; M 1437 H43/24F+20; M 1443-1447 H43/30F+15; M 1450/1 H46/30F+18; M 1481-1484 H40/36F+15) or Alexander 'RH' H43/32F+15 (M 1448/9)

Built 1978-1984

Dimensions 9563mm x 2502mm x 4382mm (M 1441/2: 9630mm x 2502mm x 4420mm)

Number Built 1485 (including 13 acquisitions from GMT, Yorkshire Rider and Busways)

Number in Stock 1443

Number Scheduled for Service 1193 (including 20 for Airbus)

1	THX101S	**63**	WYW63T	**126**	BYX126V	**186**	BYX186V	**245**	BYX245V
2	THX102S	**64**	WYW64T	**127**	BYX127V	**187**	BYX187V	**246**	BYX246V
3	THX103S	**65**	WYW65T	**128**	BYX128V	**188**	188CLT	**247**	BYX247V
4	THX104S	**66**	WYW66T	**129**	BYX129V	**189**	BYX189V	**248**	BYX248V
5	THX105S	**67**	WYW67T	**130**	BYX130V	**190**	BYX190V	**249**	BYX249V
6	WYW6T	**68**	WYW68T	**131**	BYX131V	**191**	BYX191V	**250**	BYX250V
7	WYW7T	**69**	WYW69T	**132**	BYX132V	**192**	BYX192V	**251**	BYX251V
8	WYW8T	**70**	WYW70T	**133**	BYX133V	**193**	BYX193V	**252**	BYX252V
9	WYW9T	**72**	WYW72T	**134**	BYX134V	**194**	BYX194V	**254**	BYX254V
10	WYW10T	**73**	WYW73T	**135**	BYX135V	**195**	BYX195V	**255**	BYX255V
11	WYW11T	**74**	WYW74T	**136**	BYX136V	**196**	BYX196V	**256**	BYX256V
12	WYW12T	**75**	WYW75T	**137**	BYX137V	**197**	197CLT	**257**	BYX257V
13	WYW13T	**76**	WYW76T	**138**	BYX138V	**198**	VLT98	**258**	BYX258V
14	WYW14T	**77**	WYW77T	**139**	BYX139V	**199**	BYX199V	**259**	BYX259V
15	WYW15T	**78**	WYW78T	**140**	BYX140V	**200**	BYX200V	**260**	BYX260V
16	WYW16T	**79**	WYW79T	**141**	BYX141V	**201**	BYX201V	**261**	BYX261V
17	WYW17T	**80**	WYW80T	**142**	BYX142V	**202**	BYX202V	**262**	BYX262V
18	WYW18T	**81**	WYW81T	**143**	BYX143V	**203**	BYX203V	**263**	BYX263V
19a	WYW19T	**82**	WYW82T	**144**	BYX144V	**204**	BYX204V	**264**	BYX264V
20	WYW20T	**83**	WYW83T	**145**	BYX145V	**205**	BYX205V	**265**	BYX265V
21	WYW21T	**84**	WYW84T	**146**	BYX146V	**206**	BYX206V	**266**	BYX266V
22	WYW22T	**85**	WYW85T	**147**	BYX147V	**207**	BYX207V	**267**	BYX267V
24	WYW24T	**86**a	WYW86T	**148**	BYX148V	**208**	BYX208V	**268**	BYX268V
25	WYW25T	**87**	WYW87T	**149**	BYX149V	**209**	BYX209V	**269**	BYX269V
26	WYW26T	**88**	WYW88T	**150**	BYX150V	**210**	BYX210V	**270**	BYX270V
27	WYW27T	**89**	WYW89T	**151**	BYX151V	**211**	BYX211V	**271**	BYX271V
28	WYW28T	**90**	WYW90T	**153**	BYX153V	**212**	BYX212V	**272**	BYX272V
29	WYW29T	**91**	WYW91T	**154**	BYX154V	**213**	BYX213V	**273**	BYX273V
30	WYW30T	**92**	WYW92T	**155**	BYX155V	**214**	BYX214V	**274**	BYX274V
31	WYW31T	**93**	WYW93T	**156**	BYX156V	**215**	BYX215V	**275**	BYX275V
32	WYW32T	**94**	WYW94T	**157**	BYX157V	**216**	BYX216V	**276**	BYX276V
33	WYW33T	**95**	WYW95T	**158**	BYX158V	**217**	BYX217V	**277**	BYX277V
34	WYW34T	**96**a	BYX96V	**159**	BYX159V	**218**	BYX218V	**278**	78CLT
35	WYW35T	**97**	BYX97V	**160**	BYX160V	**219**	BYX219V	**279**	BYX279V
36	WYW36T	**98**	BYX98V	**161**	BYX161X	**220**	BYX220V	**280**	BYX280V
37	WYW37T	**99**	BYX99V	**162**a	BYX162V	**221**	BYX221V	**281**	BYX281V
38	WYW38T	**100**	BYX100V	**163**	BYX163V	**222**	BYX222V	**282**	BYX282V
39a	WYW39T	**101**	BYX101V	**164**	BYX164V	**223**	BYX223V	**283**	BYX283V
40	WYW40T	**102**	BYX102V	**165**	BYX165V	**224**	BYX224V	**284**	VLT284
41	WYW41T	**103**	BYX103V	**166**	BYX166V	**225**	BYX225V	**285**	BYX285V
42	WYW42T	**106**	BYX106V	**167**	BYX167V	**226**	BYX226V	**286**	BYX286V
43a	WYW43T	**107**	BYX107V	**168**	BYX168V	**227**	BYX227V	**287**	BYX287V
44	WYW44T	**108**	BYX108V	**169**	BYX169V	**228**	BYX228V	**288**	BYX288V
45	WYW45T	**109**	BYX109V	**170**	BYX170V	**229**	BYX229V	**289**	BYX289V
46	WYW46T	**110**	BYX110V	**171**	BYX171V	**230**	BYX230V	**290**	BYX290V
47	WYW47T	**111**	BYX111V	**172**	BYX172V	**231**	BYX231V	**291**	BYX291V
48	WYW48T	**112**	BYX112V	**173**	BYX173V	**232**	BYX232V	**292**	BYX292V
49	WYW49T	**113**	BYX113V	**174**	BYX174V	**233**	BYX233V	**293**	BYX293V
51	WYW51T	**114**	BYX114V	**175**	BYX175V	**234**	BYX234V	**294**	BYX294V
52	WYW52T	**115**	BYX115V	**176**	BYX176V	**235**	BYX235V	**295**	BYX295V
54	WYW54T	**117**	BYX117V	**177**	BYX177V	**236**	BYX236V	**296**	BYX296V
55	WYW55T	**118**	BYX118V	**178**	BYX178V	**237**	BYX237V	**297**	BYX297V
56	WYW56T	**119**	BYX119V	**179**	BYX179V	**238**	BYX238V	**298**	BYX298V
57	WYW57T	**120**	BYX120V	**180**	BYX180V	**239**	BYX239V	**299**	BYX299V
58	WYW58T	**121**	BYX121V	**181**	BYX181V	**240**	BYX240V	**300**h	BYX300V
59	WYW59T	**122**	BYX122V	**182**	BYX182V	**241**	BYX241V	**301**	BYX301V
60	WYW60T	**123**	BYX123V	**183**	BYX183V	**242**	BYX242V	**302**	BYX302V
61	WYW61T	**124**	BYX124V	**184**	BYX184V	**243**	BYX243V	**303**	BYX303V
62	WYW62T	**125**	BYX125V	**185**	BYX185V	**244**	BYX244V	**304**	BYX304V

305	BYX305V	**381**	GYE381W	**457**	GYE457W	**533**	GYE533W	**609**	KYO609X
306	BYX306V	**382**	GYE382W	**458**	GYE458W	**534**	GYE534W	**610**	KYO610X
307	BYX307V	**383**	GYE383W	**459**	GYE459W	**535**	GYE535W	**611**	KYO611X
308	BYX308V	**384**	GYE384W	**460**	GYE460W	**536**	GYE536W	**612**	KYO612X
309	BYX309V	**385**	GYE385W	**461**	GYE461W	**537**	GYE537W	**613**	KYO613X
310	BYX310V	**386**	GYE386W	**462**	GYE462W	**538**	GYE538W	**614**	KYO614X
311	BYX311V	**387**	GYE387W	**463**	WLT463	**539**	GYE539W	**615**	KYO615X
312	BYX312V	**388**	GYE388W	**464**	GYE464W	**540**	GYE540W	**616**	KYO616X
313	BYX313V	**389**	GYE389W	**465**	GYE465W	**541**	GYE541W	**617**	KYO617X
314	BYX314V	**390**	GYE390W	**466**	GYE466W	**542**	542CLT	**618**	KYO618X
315	BYX315V	**391**	GYE391W	**467**	GYE467W	**543**	GYE543W	**619**	KYO619X
316	EYE316V	**392**	GYE392W	**468**	GYE468W	**544**	GYE544W	**620**	KYO620X
317	EYE317V	**393**	GYE393W	**469**	GYE469W	**545**	GYE545W	**621**	KYO621X
318	EYE318V	**394**	GYE394W	**470**	GYE470W	**546**	GYE546W	**622**	KYO622X
319	EYE319V	**395**	GYE395W	**471**	GYE471W	**547**	GYE547W	**623**	KYO623X
320	EYE320V	**396**	GYE396W	**472**	GYE472W	**548**	GYE548W	**624**	KYO624X
321	EYE321V	**397**	GYE397W	**473**	GYE473W	**549**	GYE549W	**625**	KYO625X
322	EYE322V	**398**	GYE398W	**474**	GYE474W	**550**	GYE550W	**626**	KYO626X
323	EYE323V	**399**	GYE399W	**475**	GYE475W	**551**	GYE551W	**627**	KYO627X
324	EYE324V	**400**	GYE400W	**476**	GYE476W	**552**	GYE552W	**628**	KYO628X
325	EYE325V	**401**	GYE401W	**477**	GYE477W	**553**	GYE553W	**629**	KYO629X
326	EYE326V	**402**	GYE402W	**478**	GYE478W	**554**	GYE554W	**630**	KYO630X
327	EYE327V	**403**	GYE403W	**479**	VLT179	**555**	GYE555W	**631**	KYO631X
328	EYE328V	**404**	GYE404W	**480**	GYE480W	**556**	GYE556W	**632**	KYV632X
329	EYE329V	**405**	GYE405W	**481**	GYE481W	**557**	GYE557W	**633**	KYV633X
330	EYE330V	**406**	GYE406W	**482**	GYE482W	**558**	GYE558W	**634**	KYV634X
331	EYE331V	**407**	GYE407W	**483**	GYE483W	**559**	GYE559W	**635**	KYV635X
332	EYE332V	**408**	GYE408W	**484**	GYE484W	**560**	GYE560W	**636**	KYV636X
333	EYE333V	**409**	GYE409W	**485**	GYE485W	**561**	GYE561W	**637**	KYV637X
334	EYE334V	**410**	GYE410W	**486**	GYE486W	**562**	GYE562W	**638**	KYV638X
335	EYE335V	**411**	GYE411W	**487**	GYE487W	**563**	GYE563W	**639**	KYV639X
336	EYE336V	**412**	GYE412W	**488**	GYE488W	**564**	GYE564W	**640**	KYV640X
337	EYE337V	**413**	GYE413W	**489**	GYE489W	**565**	GYE565W	**641**	KYV641X
338	EYE338V	**414**	GYE414W	**490**	GYE490W	**566**	GYE566W	**642**	KYV642X
339	EYE339V	**415**	GYE415W	**491**	GYE491W	**567**	GYE567W	**643**	KYV643X
340	EYE340V	**416**	GYE416W	**492**	GYE492W	**568**	GYE568W	**644**	KYV644X
341	EYE341V	**417**	GYE417W	**493**	GYE493W	**569**	GYE569W	**645**	KYV645X
342	EYE342V	**418**	GYE418W	**494**	GYE494W	**570**	GYE570W	**646**	KYV646X
343	EYE343V	**419**	GYE419W	**495**	GYE495W	**571**	GYE571W	**647**	KYV647X
344	EYE344V	**420**	GYE420W	**496**	GYE496W	**572**	GYE572W	**648**	KYV648X
345	EYE345V	**421**	GYE421W	**497**	GYE497W	**573**	GYE573W	**649**	KYV649X
346	GYE346W	**422**	GYE422W	**498**	GYE498W	**574**	GYE574W	**650**	KYV650X
347	GYE347W	**423**	GYE423W	**499**	GYE499W	**575**	GYE575W	**651**	KYV651X
348	GYE348W	**424**	GYE424W	**500**	GYE500W	**576**	GYE576W	**652**	KYV652X
349	GYE349W	**425**	GYE425W	**501**	GYE501W	**577**	GYE577W	**653**	KYV653X
350	GYE350W	**426**	GYE426W	**502**	GYE502W	**578**	GYE578W	**654**	KYV654X
351	GYE351W	**427**	GYE427W	**503**	GYE503W	**579**	GYE579W	**655**	KYV655X
352	GYE352W	**428**	GYE428W	**504**	GYE504W	**580**	GYE580W	**656**	KYV656X
353	GYE353W	**429**	GYE429W	**505**	GYE505W	**581**	GYE581W	**657**	KYV657X
354	GYE354W	**430**	GYE430W	**506**	GYE506W	**582**	GYE582W	**658**	KYV658X
355	GYE355W	**431**	GYE431W	**507**	GYE507W	**583**	GYE583W	**659**	KYV659X
356	GYE356W	**432**	GYE432W	**508**	GYE508W	**584**	GYE584W	**660**	KYV660X
357	GYE357W	**433**	GYE433W	**509**	GYE509W	**585**	GYE585W	**661**	KYV661X
358	GYE358W	**434**	GYE434W	**510**	GYE510W	**586**	GYE586W	**662**	KYV662X
359	GYE359W	**435**	GYE435W	**511**	GYE511W	**587**	GYE587W	**663**	KYV663X
360	GYE360W	**436**	GYE436W	**512**	GYE512W	**588**	GYE588W	**664**	KYV664X
361	GYE361W	**437**	GYE437W	**513**	GYE513W	**589**	GYE589W	**665**	KYV665X
362	GYE362W	**438**	GYE438W	**514**	GYE514W	**590**	GYE590W	**666**	KYV666X
363	GYE363W	**439**	GYE439W	**515**	GYE515W	**591**	GYE591W	**667**	KYV667X
364	GYE364W	**440**	GYE440W	**516**	GYE516W	**592**	GYE592W	**668**	KYV668X
365	GYE365W	**441**	GYE441W	**517**	GYE517W	**593**	GYE593W	**669**	KYV669X
366	GYE366W	**442**	GYE442W	**518**	GYE518W	**594**	GYE594W	**670**	KYV670X
367	GYE367W	**443**	GYE443W	**519**	GYE519W	**595**	GYE595W	**671**	KYV671X
368	GYE368W	**444**	GYE444W	**520**	GYE520W	**596**	GYE596W	**672**	KYV672X
369	GYE369W	**445**	GYE445W	**521**	GYE521W	**597**	GYE597W	**673**	KYV673X
370	GYE370W	**446**	GYE446W	**522**	GYE522W	**598**	GYE598W	**674**	KYV674X
371	GYE371W	**447**	GYE447W	**523**	GYE523W	**599**	GYE599W	**675**	KYV675X
372	GYE372W	**448**	GYE448W	**524**	GYE524W	**600**	GYE600W	**676**	KYV676X
373	GYE373W	**449**	GYE449W	**525**	GYE525W	**601**	GYE601W	**677**	KYV677X
374	GYE374W	**450**	GYE450W	**526**	GYE526W	**602**	GYE602W	**678**	KYV678X
375	GYE375W	**451**	GYE451W	**527**	GYE527W	**603**	GYE603W	**679**	KYV679X
376	GYE376W	**452**	GYE452W	**528**	GYE528W	**604**	GYE604W	**680**	KYV680X
377	GYE377W	**453**	GYE453W	**529**	GYE529W	**605**	GYE605W	**681**	KYV681X
378	GYE378W	**454**	GYE454W	**530**	GYE530W	**606**	KYO606X	**682**	KYV682X
379	WLT379	**455**	GYE455W	**531**	GYE531W	**607**	KYO607X	**683**	KYV683X
380	GYE380W	**456**	GYE456W	**532**	GYE532W	**608**	KYO608X	**684**	KYV684X

685	KYV685X	**763**	KYV763X	**839**	OJD839Y	**915**	A915SUL	**992**	A992SYF
686	KYV686X	**764**	KYV764X	**840**	OJD840Y	**916**	A916SUL	**993**	A993SYF
687	KYV687X	**765**	KYV765X	**841**	OJD841Y	**917**	A917SUL	**994**	A994SYF
688	KYV688X	**766**	KYV766X	**842**	OJD842Y	**918**	A918SUL	**995**	A995SYF
689	KYV689X	**767**	KYV767X	**843**	OJD843Y	**919**	A919SUL	**996**	A996SYF
690	KYV690X	**768**	KYV768X	**844**	OJD844Y	**920**	A920SUL	**997**	A997SYF
691	KYV691X	**769**	KYV769X	**845**	OGK708Y	**921**	A921SUL	**998**	A998SYF
692	KYV692X	**770**	KYV770X	**846**	OJD846Y	**922**	A922SUL	**999**	A999SYF
693	KYV693X	**771**	KYV771X	**847**	OJD847Y	**923**	A923SUL	**1000**	A700THV
694	KYV694X	**772**	KYV772X	**848**	OJD848Y	**924**	A924SUL	**1001**	A701THV
695	KYV695X	**773**	KYV773X	**849**	OJD849Y	**925**	A925SUL	**1002**	A702THV
696	KYV696X	**774**	KYV774X	**850**	OJD850Y	**926**	A926SUL	**1003**b	A703THV
697	KYV697X	**775**	KYV775X	**851**	OJD851Y	**927**	A927SUL	**1004**	A704THV
698	KYV698X	**776**	KYV776X	**852**	OJD852Y	**928**	A928SUL	**1005**	A705THV
699	KYV699X	**777**	KYV777X	**853**	VLT53	**929**	A929SUL	**1006**a	A706THV
700	KYV700X	**778**	KYV778X	**854**	OJD854Y	**930**	A930SUL	**1007**a	A707THV
701	KYV701X	**779**	KYV779X	**855**	OJD855Y	**931**	A931SUL	**1008**a	A708THV
702	KYV702X	**780**	KYV780X	**856**	OJD856Y	**932**	A932SUL	**1009**a	A709THV
703	KYV703X	**781**	KYV781X	**857**	OJD857Y	**933**	A933SUL	**1010**a	A710THV
704	KYV704X	**782**	KYV782X	**858**	OJD858Y	**934**	A934SUL	**1011**a	A711THV
705	KYV705X	**783**	KYV783X	**859**	OJD859Y	**935**	A935SUL	**1012**a	A712THV
706	KYV706X	**784**	KYV784X	**860**	OJD860Y	**936**	A936SUL	**1013**a	A713THV
707	KYV707X	**785**	KYV785X	**861**	OJD861Y	**937**	A937SUL	**1014**a	A714THV
708	KYV708X	**786**	KYV786X	**862**	OJD862Y	**938**	A938SUL	**1015**a	A715THV
709	KYV709X	**787**	KYV787X	**863**	OJD863Y	**939**	A939SUL	**1016**a	A716THV
710	KYV710X	**788**	KYV788X	**864**	OJD864Y	**940**	A940SUL	**1017**a	A717THV
711	KYV711X	**789**	KYV789X	**865**	OJD865Y	**941**	A941SUL	**1018**a	A718THV
712	KYV712X	**790**	KYV790X	**866**	OJD866Y	**942**	A942SUL	**1019**a	A719THV
713	KYV713X	**791**	KYV791X	**867**	OJD867Y	**943**	A943SUL	**1020**a	A720THV
714	KYV714X	**792**	KYV792X	**868**	OJD868Y	**944**	A944SUL	**1021**a	A721THV
715	KYV715X	**793**	KYV793X	**869**	OJD869Y	**945**	A945SUL	**1022**a	A722THV
716	KYV716X	**794**	KYV794X	**870**	OJD870Y	**946**	A947SUL	**1023**a	A723THV
717	KYV717X	**795**	KYV795X	**871**	OJD871Y	**947**	A947SUL	**1024**a	A724THV
718	KYV718X	**796**	KYV796X	**872**	OJD872Y	**948**	A948SUL	**1025**a	A725THV
719	KYV719X	**797**	KYV797X	**873**	OJD873Y	**949**	A949SUL	**1026**a	A726THV
720	KYV720X	**798**	KYV798X	**874**	OJD874Y	**950**	A950SUL	**1027**a	A727THV
721	KYV721X	**799**	KYV799X	**875**	OJD875Y	**951**	A951SUL	**1028**a	A728THV
722	KYV722X	**800**	KYV800X	**876**	OJD876Y	**952**	A952SUL	**1029**a	A729THV
723	KYV723X	**801**	KYV801X	**877**	OJD877Y	**953**	A953SUL	**1030**	A730THV
724	KYV724X	**802**	KYV802X	**878**	OJD878Y	**954**	WLT954	**1031**	A731THV
725	KYV725X	**803**	KYV803X	**879**	OJD879Y	**955**	A955SUL	**1032**	A732THV
726	KYV726X	**804**o	KYV804X	**880**	OJD880Y	**956**	A956SYF	**1033**	A733THV
727	KYV727X	**805**	KYV805X	**881**	OJD881Y	**957**	A957SYF	**1034**	A734THV
728	KYV728X	**806**	OJD806Y	**882**	OJD882Y	**958**	A958SYF	**1035**	A735THV
729	KYV729X	**807**	OJD807Y	**883**	OJD883Y	**959**	A959SYF	**1036**	A736THV
730	KYV730X	**808**	OJD808Y	**884**	OJD884Y	**960**	A960SYF	**1037**	A737THV
731	KYV731X	**809**	OJD809Y	**885**	OJD885Y	**961**	A961SYF	**1038**	A738THV
732	KYV732X	**810**	OJD810Y	**886**	OJD886Y	**962**	A962SYF	**1039**	A739THV
733	KYV733X	**811**	OJD811Y	**887**	OJD887Y	**963**	A963SYF	**1040**	A740THV
734	KYV734X	**812**	OJD812Y	**888**	OJD888Y	**964**	A964SYF	**1041**	A741THV
736	KYV736X	**813**	OJD813Y	**889**	OJD889Y	**965**	A965SYF	**1042**	A742THV
737	KYV737X	**814**	OJD814Y	**890**	OJD890Y	**966**	A966SYF	**1043**	A743THV
738	KYV738X	**815**	OJD815Y	**891**	OJD891Y	**967**	A967SYF	**1044**	A744THV
739	KYV739X	**816**	OJD816Y	**892**	A892SUL	**968**	A968SYF	**1045**b	A745THV
740	KYV740X	**817**	OJD817Y	**893**	A893SUL	**969**	A969SYF	**1046**	VLT46
741	KYV741X	**818**	OJD818Y	**894**	A894SUL	**970**	A970SYF	**1047**	A747THV
742	KYV742X	**819**	OJD819Y	**895**	A895SUL	**971**	A971SYF	**1048**	A748THV
743	KYV743X	**820**	OJD820Y	**896**	A896SUL	**972**	A972SYF	**1049**	A749THV
744	KYV744X	**821**	OJD821Y	**897**	A897SUL	**973**	A973SYF	**1050**	A750THV
745	KYV745X	**822**	OJD822Y	**898**	A898SUL	**974**	A974SYF	**1051**	A751THV
746	KYV746X	**823**	OJD823Y	**899**	A899SUL	**975**	A975SYF	**1052**	A752THV
747	KYV747X	**824**	OJD824Y	**900**	A900SUL	**976**	A976SYF	**1053**	A753THV
748	KYV748X	**825**	OJD825Y	**901**	A901SUL	**977**	A977SYF	**1054**	A754THV
749	KYV749X	**826**	OJD826Y	**902**	A902SUL	**978**	A978SYF	**1055**	A755THV
750	KYV750X	**827**	OJD827Y	**903**	A903SUL	**979**	A979SYF	**1056**	B56WUL
751	KYV751X	**828**	OJD828Y	**904**	A904SUL	**980**	A980SYF	**1057**	B57WUL
752	KYV752X	**829**	OJD829Y	**905**	A905SUL	**981**	A981SYF	**1058**	B58WUL
753	KYV753X	**830**	OJD830Y	**906**	A906SUL	**982**	A982SYF	**1059**	B59WUL
754	KYV754X	**831**	OJD831Y	**907**	A907SUL	**983**	A983SYF	**1060**	B60WUL
755	KYV755X	**832**	OJD832Y	**908**	A908SUL	**984**	A984SYF	**1061**	B61WUL
756	KYV756X	**833**	OJD833Y	**909**	A909SUL	**985**	A985SYF	**1062**	B62WUL
757	KYV757X	**834**	OJD834Y	**910**	A910SUL	**987**	A987SYF	**1063**	B63WUL
758	KYV758X	**835**	OJD835Y	**911**	A911SUL	**988**	A988SYF	**1064**	B64WUL
760	KYV760X	**836**	OJD836Y	**912**	A912SUL	**989**	A989SYF	**1065**	B65WUL
761	KYV761X	**837**	OJD837Y	**913**	A913SUL	**990**	A990SYF	**1066**	B66WUL
762	KYV762X	**838**	OJD838Y	**914**	A914SUL	**991**	A991SYF	**1067**	B67WUL

a Airbus livery b High-back seating d Gardner turbocharged engine g London United livery o Open top

1068	B68WUL	**1146**	B146WUL	**1224**	B224WUL	**1302**	B302WUL	**1380**	C380BUV
1069g	B69WUL	**1147**	B147WUL	**1225**	B225WUL	**1303**	B303WUL	**1381**	C381BUV
1070	B70WUL	**1148**	B148WUL	**1226**	B226WUL	**1304**	B304WUL	**1382**	C382BUV
1071	B71WUL	**1149**	B149WUL	**1227**	B227WUL	**1305**	B305WUL	**1383**	C383BUV
1072	B72WUL	**1150**	B150WUL	**1228**	B228WUL	**1306**	C306BUV	**1384**	C384BUV
1073	B73WUL	**1151**	B151WUL	**1229**	B229WUL	**1307**	C307BUV	**1385**	C385BUV
1074	B74WUL	**1152**	B152WUL	**1230**	B230WUL	**1308**	C308BUV	**1386**	C386BUV
1075	B75WUL	**1153**	B153WUL	**1231**	B231WUL	**1309**	C309BUV	**1387**	C387BUV
1076	B76WUL	**1154**	B154WUL	**1232**	B232WUL	**1310**	C310BUV	**1388**	C388BUV
1077	B77WUL	**1155**	B155WUL	**1233**	B233WUL	**1311**	C311BUV	**1389**	89CLT
1078	B78WUL	**1156**	B156WUL	**1234**	B234WUL	**1312**	C312BUV	**1390**	C390BUV
1079	B79WUL	**1157**	B157WUL	**1235**	B235WUL	**1313**	C313BUV	**1391**	C391BUV
1080	B80WUL	**1158**	B158WUL	**1236**	B236WUL	**1314**	C314BUV	**1392**	C392BUV
1081	B81WUL	**1159**	B159WUL	**1237**	B237WUL	**1315**	VLT15	**1393**b	C393BUV
1082	B82WUL	**1160**	B160WUL	**1238**	B238WUL	**1316**	C316BUV	**1394**	C394BUV
1083	B83WUL	**1161**	B161WUL	**1239**	B239WUL	**1317**	C317BUV	**1395**	C395BUV
1084	B84WUL	**1162**	B162WUL	**1240**	B240WUL	**1318**	C318BUV	**1396**b	C396BUV
1085	B85WUL	**1163**	B163WUL	**1241**	B241WUL	**1319**	C319BUV	**1397**	C397BUV
1086	B86WUL	**1164**	B164WUL	**1242**	B242WUL	**1320**	C320BUV	**1398**b	C398BUV
1087	B87WUL	**1165**	B165WUL	**1243**	B243WUL	**1321**	C321BUV	**1399**	C399BUV
1088	B88WUL	**1166**	B166WUL	**1244**	B244WUL	**1322**	C322BUV	**1400**	C400BUV
1089	B89WUL	**1167**	B167WUL	**1245**	B245WUL	**1323**	C323BUV	**1401**	C401BUV
1090	B90WUL	**1168**	B168WUL	**1246**	B246WUL	**1324**	C324BUV	**1402**	C402BUV
1091	B91WUL	**1169**	B169WUL	**1247**	B247WUL	**1325**	C325BUV	**1403**	C403BUV
1092	B92WUL	**1170**	B170WUL	**1248**	B248WUL	**1326**	C326BUV	**1404**	C404BUV
1093	B93WUL	**1171**	B171WUL	**1249**	B249WUL	**1327**	C327BUV	**1405**	C405BUV
1094	B94WUL	**1172**	B172WUL	**1250**	B250WUL	**1328**	C328BUV	**1406**	C406BUV
1095	B95WUL	**1173**	B173WUL	**1251**b	B251WUL	**1329**	C329BUV	**1407**	C407BUV
1096	B96WUL	**1174**	B174WUL	**1252**	B252WUL	**1330**	C330BUV	**1408**	C408BUV
1097	B97WUL	**1175**	B175WUL	**1253**	B253WUL	**1331**	C331BUV	**1409**	C409BUV
1098	B98WUL	**1176**	B176WUL	**1254**	B254WUL	**1332**	C332BUV	**1410**	C410BUV
1099	B99WUL	**1177**	B177WUL	**1255**	B255WUL	**1333**	C333BUV	**1411**	C411BUV
1100	B100WUL	**1178**	B178WUL	**1256**	B256WUL	**1334**	C334BUV	**1412**	C412BUV
1101	B101WUL	**1179**	B179WUL	**1257**	B257WUL	**1335**	C335BUV	**1413**	C413BUV
1102	B102WUL	**1180**	B180WUL	**1258**	B258WUL	**1336**	C336BUV	**1414**	C414BUV
1103	B103WUL	**1181**	B181WUL	**1259**	B259WUL	**1337**	C337BUV	**1415**	C415BUV
1104	B104WUL	**1182**	B182WUL	**1260**	B260WUL	**1338**	C338BUV	**1416**	C416BUV
1105	B105WUL	**1183**	B183WUL	**1261**	B261WUL	**1339**	C339BUV	**1417**	C417BUV
1106	B106WUL	**1184**	B184WUL	**1262**	B262WUL	**1340**	C340BUV	**1418**	C418BUV
1107	B107WUL	**1185**	B185WUL	**1263**	B263WUL	**1341**	C341BUV	**1419**	C419BUV
1108	B108WUL	**1186**	B186WUL	**1264**	B264WUL	**1342**	C342BUV	**1420**	C420BUV
1109	B109WUL	**1187**	B187WUL	**1265**	B265WUL	**1343**	C343BUV	**1421**	C421BUV
1110	B110WUL	**1188**	B188WUL	**1266**	B266WUL	**1344**	C344BUV	**1422**	C422BUV
1111	B111WUL	**1189**	B189WUL	**1267**	B267WUL	**1345**	C345BUV	**1423**	C423BUV
1112	B112WUL	**1190**	B190WUL	**1268**	B268WUL	**1346**	C346BUV	**1424**	C424BUV
1113	B113WUL	**1191**	B191WUL	**1269**	B269WUL	**1347**	C347BUV	**1425**	C425BUV
1114	B114WUL	**1192**	B192WUL	**1270**	B270WUL	**1348**	C348BUV	**1426**	C426BUV
1115	B115WUL	**1193**	B193WUL	**1271**	B271WUL	**1349**	C349BUV	**1427**	C427BUV
1116	B116WUL	**1194**	B194WUL	**1272**	B272WUL	**1350**	C350BUV	**1428**	C428BUV
1117	B117WUL	**1195**	B195WUL	**1273**	B273WUL	**1351**	C351BUV	**1429**	C429BUV
1118	B118WUL	**1196**	B196WUL	**1274**	B274WUL	**1352**	C352BUV	**1430**	C430BUV
1119	B119WUL	**1197**	B197WUL	**1275**	B275WUL	**1353**	C353BUV	**1431**	C431BUV
1120	B120WUL	**1198**	B198WUL	**1276**	B276WUL	**1354**	C354BUV	**1432**b	WLT432
1121	B121WUL	**1199**	B199WUL	**1277**	B277WUL	**1355**	C355BUV	**1433**	C433BUV
1122	B122WUL	**1200**	B200WUL	**1278**	B278WUL	**1356**	C356BUV	**1434**	WLT434
1123	B123WUL	**1201**	B201WUL	**1279**	B279WUL	**1357**	C357BUV	**1435**	435CLT
1124	B124WUL	**1202**	B202WUL	**1280**	B280WUL	**1358**	C358BUV	**1436**	VLT136
1125	B125WUL	**1203**	B203WUL	**1281**	B281WUL	**1359**	C359BUV	**1437**bd	VLT12
1126	B126WUL	**1204**	B204WUL	**1282**	B282WUL	**1360**	C360BUV	**1438**	C438BUV
1127	B127WUL	**1205**	B205WUL	**1283**	B283WUL	**1361**	C361BUV	**1439**	C439BUV
1128	B128WUL	**1206**	B206WUL	**1284**	B284WUL	**1362**	C362BUV	**1440**	C440BUV
1129	B129WUL	**1207**	B207WUL	**1285**	B285WUL	**1363**	C363BUV	**1441**	A441UUV
1130	B130WUL	**1208**	B208WUL	**1286**	B286WUL	**1364**	C364BUV	**1442**	A442UUV
1131	B131WUL	**1209**	B209WUL	**1287**	B287WUL	**1365**	C365BUV	**1443**	GBU1V
1132	B132WUL	**1210**	B210WUL	**1288**	B288WUL	**1366**	C366BUV	**1444**	GBU4V
1133	B133WUL	**1211**	B211WUL	**1289**	B289WUL	**1367**b	C367BUV	**1445**	GBU5V
1134	B134WUL	**1212**	B212WUL	**1290**	B290WUL	**1368**	C368BUV	**1446**	GBU8V
1135	B135WUL	**1213**	B213WUL	**1291**	B291WUL	**1369**	C369BUV	**1447**	GBU9V
1136	B136WUL	**1214**	B214WUL	**1292**	B292WUL	**1370**	C370BUV	**1448**	UWW518X
1137	B137WUL	**1215**	B215WUL	**1293**	B293WUL	**1371**	C371BUV	**1449**	UWW519X
1138	B138WUL	**1216**	B216WUL	**1294**	B294WUL	**1372**	C372BUV	**1450**	CUB539Y
1139	B139WUL	**1217**	B217WUL	**1295**	B295WUL	**1373**	C373BUV	**1451**	CUB540Y
1140	B140WUL	**1218**	B218WUL	**1296**	B296WUL	**1374**	C374BUV	**1481**	VRG415T
1141	B141WUL	**1219**	B219WUL	**1297**	B297WUL	**1375**	C375BUV	**1482**	VRG416T
1142	B142WUL	**1220**	B220WUL	**1298**	B298WUL	**1376**	C376BUV	**1483**	VRG417T
1143	B143WUL	**1221**	B221WUL	**1299**	B299WUL	**1377**	C377BUV	**1484**	VRG418T
1144	B144WUL	**1222**	B222WUL	**1300**	B300WUL	**1378**	C378BUV		
1145	B145WUL	**1223**	B223WUL	**1301**	B301WUL	**1379**b	VLT88		

Named vehicles: M 1367 *Senator*, M 1398 *Ambassador*

T **Sub-frames** Leyland Titan TNLXB2RRSp (T 261, 877/80 are TNTL112RRSp and T 345, 881-3/5 are TNL112RRSp subsequently modified to TNLXB2RRSp specification; T 1126-1130 are TNLXB1RF)

Engine Gardner 6LXB 10.45-litre rated at 1217kW at 1850rpm

Bodywork Park Royal (T 1-250, 1126-30) or Leyland/Park Royal (T 251-263) or Leyland (T 264-1125)

Capacity H44/24D+21 (T 1, 3-8, 13-8, 21/3/4/7-9, 31/2/4/5/7/8, 49, 64, 78, 88/9, 91/4/7/9 H44/22D+21; T 2, 9-12/9, 20/2/5/6, 30/3/6/9, 40/2/4-6/8, 50/1/3/4/6-8/62/6/7/9-71/4-6/9, 83-6, 90/2/3/5/8, 100/6/21/2/30/40/2/3/9/52-4/6-8/60-4/9-73/5/6/8/81/5-9/91/3/5-8, 202/7/8/10/4-6/22/3/6/8/9/33/5-7/40-8/50-4/60-3/5/6/75/82/5/7/90, 300/1/9/11/7/20-2/31/45, 799-802/4-1059/61-125 H44/26D+21; T 63, 80, 1063 H44/26F+21; T 512 O44/24D+21; T 803 O44/26D+21; T 1126-1130 CH43/29F+10)

Built 1977-1984

Dimensions 9566mm x 2502mm x 4382mm

Number Built 1131 (including acquisitions)

Number in Stock 964

Number Scheduled for Service 685

1	THX401S	**62**	WYV62T	**154**	CUL154V	**240**	EYE240V	**314**	KYV314X
2	THX402S	**63**s	WYV63T	**156**	CUL156V	**242**z	EYE242V	**315**t	KYV315X
3	WYV3T	**64**	WYV64T	**157**	CUL157V	**243**z	EYE243V	**316**	KYV316X
4	WYV4T	**66**	WYV66T	**158**t	CUL158V	**244**	EYE244V	**317**	KYV317X
5	WYV5T	**67**	WYV67T	**160**	CUL160V	**245**	EYE245V	**318**	KYV318X
6	WYV6T	**69**	CUL69V	**163**	CUL163V	**246**	EYE246V	**319**	KYV319X
7	WYV7T	**71**	CUL71V	**164**	CUL164V	**248**	EYE248V	**320**	KYV320X
8	WYV8T	**74**	CUL74V	**168**	CUL168V	**250**	EYE250V	**321**	KYV321X
9	WYV9T	**75**	CUL75V	**169**	CUL169V	**251**	GYE251W	**322**	KYV322X
10	WYV10T	**76**	CUL76V	**170**	CUL170V	**252**	GYE252W	**323**	KYV323X
11	WYV11T	**78**	CUL78V	**171**	CUL171V	**254**	GYE254W	**325**	KYV325X
12	WYV12T	**79**	CUL79V	**172**	CUL172V	**258**	GYE258W	**326**	KYV326X
13	WYV13T	**80**s	CUL80V	**173**	CUL173V	**260**	GYE260W	**327**	KYV327X
14	WYV14T	**83**u	CUL83V	**175**t	CUL175V	†**261**	GYE261W	**328**	KYV328X
15	WYV15T	**85**	CUL85V	**176**	CUL176V	**262**	GYE262W	**329**	KYV329X
16	WYV16T	**86**t	CUL86V	**178**	CUL178V	**263**	GYE263W	**330**	KYV330X
17	WYV17T	**88**	CUL88V	**179**	CUL179V	**264**	GYE264W	**331**	KYV331X
18	WYV18T	**89**	CUL89V	**180**	CUL180V	**265**k	GYE265W	**333**t	KYV333X
19	WYV19T	**90**	CUL90V	**181**	CUL181V	**266**	GYE266W	**334**	KYV334X
20	WYV20T	**91**	CUL91V	**185**u	CUL185V	**267**	GYE267W	**335**	KYV335X
21	WYV21T	**92**	CUL92V	**186**	CUL186V	**268**	GYE268W	**336**	KYV336X
22	WYV22T	**93**	CUL93V	**189**	CUL189V	**270**	GYE270W	**337**t	KYV337X
23	WYV23T	**94**	CUL94V	**190**	CUL190V	**271**t	GYE271W	**340**	KYV340X
24	WYV24T	**95**u	CUL95V	**191**	CUL191V	**272**	GYE272W	**341**	KYV341X
25	WYV25T	**97**	CUL97V	**193**t	CUL193V	**273**	GYE273W	**342**t	KYV342X
26	WYV26T	**98**	CUL98V	**195**u	CUL195V	**274**	GYE274W	**343**	KYV343X
27	WYV27T	**99**	CUL99V	**197**	CUL197V	**275**	GYE275W	**344**u	KYV344X
28	WYV28T	**100**u	CUL100V	**198**	CUL198V	**279**t	GYE279W	**345**	KYV345X
29	WYV29T	**101**	CUL101V	**202**	CUL202V	**281**	GYE281W	**346**k	KYV346X
30	WYV30T	**103**	CUL103V	**205**t	CUL205V	**282**	KYN282X	**348**	KYV348X
31	WYV31T	**106**	CUL106V	**207**u	CUL207V	**285**	KYN285X	**349**t	KYV349X
32	WYV32T	**110**	CUL110V	**208**	CUL208V	**286**	KYN286X	**352**	KYV352X
33	WYV33T	**114**t	CUL114V	**209**	CUL209V	**287**	KYN287X	**356**	KYV356X
34	WYV34T	**116**	CUL116V	**210**t	CUL210V	**288**	KYN288X	**357**	KYV357X
35	WYV35T	**117**u	CUL117V	**212**	CUL212V	**290**	KYN290X	**358**t	KYV358X
36	WYV36T	**120**t	CUL120V	**214**t	CUL214V	**291**	KYN291X	**360**	KYV360X
37	WYV37T	**121**	CUL121V	**215**	CUL215V	**292**	KYN292X	**361**	KYV361X
38	WYV38T	**122**	CUL122V	**216**	CUL216V	**294**	KYN294X	**362**	KYV362X
39	WYV39T	**126**	CUL126V	**221**	CUL22†V	**295**	KYN295X	**363**t	KYV363X
40	WYV40T	**128**	CUL128V	**222**	CUL222V	**297**	KYN297X	**364**	KYV364X
42	WYV42T	**129**	CUL129V	**223**t	CUL223V	**298**	KYN298X	**365**t	KYV365X
44	WYV44T	**130**t	CUL130V	**224**t	CUL224V	**300**	KYN300X	**366**	KYV366X
45z	WYV45T	**133**	CUL133V	**225**	CUL225V	**301**u	KYN301X	**367**u	KYV367X
46	WYV46T	**134**	CUL134V	**226**	EYE226V	**302**	KYN302X	**368**	KYV368X
48	WYV48T	**135**	CUL135V	**227**	EYE227V	**305**	KYN305X	**369**	KYV369X
49	WYV49T	**137**t	CUL137V	**228**	EYE228V	**306**	KYN306X	**370**	KYV370X
50	WYV50T	**139**	CUL139V	**229**	EYE229V	**307**t	KYN307X	**371**t	KYV371X
51	WYV51T	**140**	CUL140V	**230**t	EYE230V	**308**	KYN308X	**372**	KYV372X
53	WYV53T	**142**t	CUL142V	**233**	EYE233V	**309**	KYN309X	**373**	KYV373X
54	WYV54T	**143**	CUL143V	**235**	EYE235V	**310**	KYN310X	**374**	KYV374X
56	WYV56T	**149**	CUL149V	**236**	EYE236V	**311**	KYV311X	**375**	KYV375X
57	WYV57T	**152**	CUL152V	**237**	EYE237V	**312**	KYV312X	**376**	KYV376X
58z	WYV58T	**153**	CUL153V	**238**t	EYE238V	**313**	KYV313X	**377**	KYV377X

† TL11 engine k Westlink livery t Trainer u Unlicensed z Permanent trainer (classified TT)

378	KYV378X	**474**	KYV474X	**551**	NUW551Y	**627**	NUW627Y	**701**	OHV701Y
379	KYV379X	**475**	KYV475X	**552**	NUW552Y	**628**	NUW628Y	**702**	OHV702Y
380	KYV380X	**476**	KYV476X	**553**	NUW553Y	**629**	NUW629Y	**704**	OHV704Y
381	KYV381X	**477**	KYV477X	**554**	NUW554Y	**630**	NUW630Y	**705**	OHV705Y
382	KYV382X	**478**	KYV478X	**555**	NUW555Y	**631**	NUW631Y	**707**	OHV707Y
384	KYV384X	**479**	KYV479X	**556**	NUW556Y	**632**	NUW632Y	**709**	OHV709Y
386	KYV386X	**480**	KYV480X	**557**	NUW557Y	**633**	NUW633Y	**710**	OHV710Y
387	KYV387X	**481**	KYV481X	**558**	NUW558Y	**634**	NUW634Y	**711**	OHV711Y
388	KYV388X	**482**	KYV482X	**559**	NUW559Y	**635**	NUW635Y	**712**	OHV712Y
390	KYV390X	**483**	KYV483X	**560**	NUW560Y	**636**	NUW636Y	**713**	OHV713Y
392	KYV392X	**485**	KYV485X	**562**	NUW562Y	**637**	NUW637Y	**714**	OHV714Y
393	KYV393X	**486**	KYV486X	**563**	NUW563Y	**638**	NUW638Y	**715**	OHV715Y
394	KYV394X	**487**	KYV487X	**564**	NUW564Y	**639**	NUW639Y	**716**	OHV716Y
395	KYV395X	**488**	KYV488X	**565**	NUW565Y	**640**	NUW640Y	**717**	OHV717Y
396	KYV396X	**490**	KYV490X	**566**	NUW566Y	**641**	NUW641Y	**718**	OHV718Y
397	KYV397X	**492**	KYV492X	**567**	NUW567Y	**642**	NUW642Y	**719**	OHV719Y
399	KYV399X	**493**	KYV493X	**568**	NUW568Y	**643**	NUW643Y	**720**	OHV720Y
401	KYV401X	**494**	KYV494X	**569**	NUW569Y	**644**	NUW644Y	**721**	OHV721Y
403	KYV403X	**495**	KYV495X	**570**	NUW570Y	**645**	NUW645Y	**722**	OHV722Y
404	KYV404X	**496**	KYV496X	**571**	NUW571Y	**646**	NUW646Y	**723**	OHV723Y
405	KYV405X	**497**	KYV497X	**572**	NUW573Y	**647**	NUW647Y	**724**	OHV724Y
406	KYV406X	**498**	KYV498X	**574**	NUW574Y	**648**	NUW648Y	**725**	OHV725Y
407	KYV407X	**499**w	KYV499X	**575**	NUW575Y	**649**	NUW649Y	**727**	OHV727Y
408	KYV408X	**500**	KYV500X	**576**	NUW576Y	**650**	NUW650Y	**728**	OHV728Y
410	KYV410X	**501**	KYV501X	**577**	NUW577Y	**651**	NUW651Y	**729**u	OHV729Y
411	KYV411X	**502**	KYV502X	**578**	NUW578Y	**652**	NUW652Y	**731**	OHV731Y
415	KYV415X	**503**	KYV503X	**579**	NUW579Y	**653**	NUW653Y	**732**	OHV732Y
419	KYV419X	**504**	KYV504X	**580**	NUW580Y	**654**	NUW654Y	**733**	OHV733Y
420	KYV420X	**505**	KYV505X	**581**	NUW581Y	**656**	NUW656Y	**735**	OHV735Y
422	KYV422X	**506**	KYV506X	**582**	NUW582Y	**657**	NUW657Y	**736**	OHV736Y
423	KYV423X	**507**	KYV507X	**583**	NUW583Y	**658**	NUW658Y	**737**	OHV737Y
424w	KYV424X	**508**	KYV508X	**584**	NUW584Y	**659**	NUW659Y	**738**	OHV738Y
428	KYV428X	**510**	KYV510X	**585**	NUW585Y	**660**	NUW660Y	**739**	OHV739Y
429	KYV429X	**511**	KYV511X	**586**	NUW586Y	**661**	NUW661Y	**740**	OHV740Y
432	KYV432X	**512**at	KYV512X	**587**	NUW587Y	**662**	NUW662Y	**741**	OHV741Y
433	KYV433X	**513**	KYV513X	**588**	NUW588Y	**663**	NUW663Y	**742**	OHV742Y
434	KYV434X	**514**	KYV514X	**589**	NUW589Y	**664**	NUW664Y	**743**	OHV743Y
435	KYV435X	**515**	KYV515X	**590**	NUW590Y	**665**	NUW665Y	**744**	OHV744Y
436	KYV436X	**516**	KYV516X	**591**	NUW591Y	**666**	NUW666Y	**745**	OHV745Y
437	KYV437X	**517**	KYV517X	**592**	NUW592Y	**667**	NUW667Y	**746**	OHV746Y
438	KYV438X	**518**	KYV518X	**593**	NUW593Y	**668**	NUW668Y	**747**	OHV747Y
439	KYV439X	**519**	KYV519X	**594**	NUW594Y	**669**	NUW669Y	**748**	OHV748Y
441	KYV441X	**520**	KYV520X	**595**	NUW595Y	**670**	NUW670Y	**749**	OHV749Y
442	KYV442X	**521**	KYV521X	**596**	NUW596Y	**671**	NUW671Y	**750**	OHV750Y
443	KYV443X	**522**	KYV522X	**597**	NUW597Y	**672**	NUW672Y	**751**	OHV751Y
444	KYV444X	**523**	KYV523X	**598**	NUW598Y	**673**	NUW673Y	**752**	OHV752Y
445	KYV445X	**524**	KYV524X	**600**	NUW600Y	**674**	NUW674Y	**753**	OHV753Y
446	KYV446X	**525**	KYV525X	**601**	NUW601Y	**675**	NUW675Y	**755**	OHV755Y
447	KYV447X	**526**	KYV526X	**602**	NUW602Y	**676**	OHV676Y	**756**	OHV756Y
448	KYV448X	**527**	KYV527X	**603**	NUW603Y	**677**	OHV677Y	**757**	OHV757Y
450	KYV450X	**529**	KYV529X	**604**	NUW604Y	**678**	OHV678Y	**759**	OHV759Y
451	KYV451X	**530**	KYV530X	**605**	NUW605Y	**679**	OHV679Y	**760**	OHV760Y
452	KYV452X	**531**	KYV531X	**606**	NUW606Y	**680**	OHV680Y	**761**	OHV761Y
453	KYV453X	**532**	KYV532X	**607**	NUW607Y	**681**	OHV681Y	**762**	OHV762Y
454	KYV454X	**533**	KYV533X	**608**	NUW608Y	**683**	OHV683Y	**763**	OHV763Y
455	KYV455X	**534**	KYV534X	**609**	NUW609Y	**684**	OHV684Y	**764**	OHV764Y
456	KYV456X	**535**	KYV535X	**610**	NUW610Y	**685**	OHV685Y	**765**	OHV765Y
457	KYV457X	**536**	KYV536X	**611**	NUW611Y	**686**	OHV686Y	**766**	OHV766Y
458	KYV458X	**537**	KYV537X	**613**	NUW613Y	**687**	OHV687Y	**767**	OHV767Y
459	KYV459X	**538**	KYV538X	**614**	NUW614Y	**688**u	OHV688Y	**768**	OHV768Y
460	KYV460X	**539**	KYV539X	**615**	NUW615Y	**689**	OHV689Y	**769**	OHV769Y
461	KYV461X	**540**	KYV540X	**616**	NUW616Y	**691**u	OHV691Y	**770**	OHV770Y
462	KYV462X	**541**	KYV541X	**617**	NUW617Y	**692**	OHV692Y	**771**	OHV771Y
464	KYV464X	**542**	KYV542X	**618**	NUW618Y	**693**	OHV693Y	**772**	OHV772Y
465	KYV465X	**543**	KYV543X	**619**	NUW619Y	**694**	OHV694Y	**773**	OHV773Y
466	KYV466X	**544**	KYV544X	**621**	NUW621Y	**695**	OHV695Y	**774**	OHV774Y
467	KYV467X	**545**	KYV545X	**622**	NUW622Y	**696**	OHV696Y	**775**	OHV775Y
469	KYV469X	**546**	KYV546X	**623**	NUW623Y	**697**	OHV697Y	**776**	OHV776Y
470	KYV470X	**548**	KYV548X	**624**	NUW624Y	**698**	OHV698Y	**778**	OHV778Y
471	KYV471X	**549**	KYV549X	**625**	NUW625Y	**699**	OHV699Y	**779**	OHV779Y
473	KYV473X	**550**	NUW550Y	**626**	NUW626Y	**700**	OHV700Y	**780**	OHV780Y

o Open top t Trainer u Unlicensed w Withdrawn

781	OHV781Y	**851**	A851SUL	**924**	A924SYE	**993**	A993SYE	**1063**s	A63THX
782	OHV782Y	**852**	A852SUL	**925**	A925SYE	**994**	A994SYE	**1064**	A64THX
783	OHV783Y	**853**	A853SUL	**926**	A926SYE	**995**	A995SYE	**1065**	A65THX
784	OHV784Y	**854**	A854SUL	**927**	A927SYE	**996**	A996SYE	**1066**	A66THX
785	OHV785Y	**855**	A855SUL	**928**	A928SYE	**997**	A997SYE	**1067**	A67THX
786	OHV786Y	**856**	A856SUL	**929**	A929SYE	**998**k	A998SYE	**1068**	A68THX
787	OHV787Y	**857**	A857SUL	**930**	A930SYE	**999**	A999SYE	**1070**	A70THX
788	OHV788Y	**858**	A858SUL	**931**	A931SYE	**1000**	ALM1B	**1071**	A71THX
789u	OHV789Y	**859**	A859SUL	**932**	A932SYE	**1001**	A601THV	**1072**	A72THX
790	OHV790Y	**860**	A860SUL	**933**	A933SYE	**1002**	A602THV	**1073**	A73THX
791	OHV791Y	**861**k	A861SUL	**934**k	A934SYE	**1003**	A603THV	**1074**	A74THX
792	OHV792Y	**862**ku	A862SUL	**935**ku	A935SYE	**1004**	A604THV	**1075**	A75THX
793	OHV793Y	**863**	A863SUL	**936**	A936SYE	**1005**	A605THV	**1076**	A76THX
794	OHV794Y	**864**	A864SUL	**937**	A937SYE	**1006**	A606THV	**1077**	A77THX
795	OHV795Y	**865**k	A865SUL	**938**	A938SYE	**1007**	A607THV	**1078**	A78THX
796	OHV796Y	**866**	A866SUL	**939**	A939SYE	**1008**c	A608THV	**1079**	B79WUV
797	OHV797Y	**867**	A867SUL	**940**	A940SYE	**1009**	A609THV	**1080**	B80WUV
798	OHV798Y	**868**	A868SUL	**941**	A941SYE	**1010**	A610THV	**1081**	B81WUV
799	OHV799Y	**869**	A869SUL	**942**	A942SYE	**1011**	A611THV	**1082**	B82WUV
800	OHV800Y	**870**	A870SUL	**943**	A943SYE	**1012**	A612THV	**1083**	B83WUV
801	OHV801Y	**871**	A871SUL	**944**k	A944SYE	**1013**	A613THV	**1084**	B84WUV
802u	OHV802Y	**872**ku	A872SUL	**945**ku	A945SYE	**1014**	A614THV	**1085**	B85WUV
803ou	OHV803Y	**873**	A873SUL	**946**	A946SYE	**1015**	A615THV	**1086**	B86WUV
804	OHV804Y	**874**	A874SUL	**947**	A947SYE	**1016**	A616THV	**1087**	B87WUV
805	OHV805Y	**875**	A875SUL	**948**	A948SYE	**1017**	A617THV	**1088**	B88WUV
806	OHV806Y	**876**	A876SUL	**949**	A949SYE	**1018**	A618THV	**1089**	B89WUV
807k	OHV807Y	**877**	A877SUL	**950**	A950SYE	**1019**	A619THV	**1090**	B90WUV
808	OHV808Y	**880**	A880SUL	**951**	A951SYE	**1020**	A620THV	**1091**	B91WUV
809	OHV809Y	**881**u	A881SUL	**952**	A952SYE	**1021**	A621THV	**1092**	B92WUV
810	OHV810Y	**882**	A882SUL	**953**ku	A953SYE	**1022**	A622THV	**1093**	B93WUV
811	OHV811Y	**883**	A883SUL	**954**	A954SYE	**1023**	A623THV	**1094**	B94WUV
812	OHV812Y	**885**	A885SUL	**955**	A955SYE	**1024**	A624THV	**1095**	B95WUV
813	OHV813Y	**886**	A886SYE	**956**	A956SYE	**1025**	A625THV	**1096**	B96WUV
814	OHV814Y	**887**	A887SYE	**957**	A957SYE	**1026**	A626THV	**1097**	B97WUV
815	OHV815Y	**888**	A888SYE	**958**	A958SYE	**1027**	A627THV	**1098**	B98WUV
816	RYK816Y	**889**	A889SYE	**959**	A959SYE	**1028**	A628THV	**1099**	B99WUV
818	RYK818Y	**890**	A890SYE	**960**u	A960SYE	**1029**	A629THV	**1100**	B100WUV
819	RYK819Y	**891**	A891SYE	**961**	A961SYE	**1030**	A630THV	**1101**	B101WUV
820	RYK820Y	**892**	A892SYE	**962**	A962SYE	**1031**	A631THV	**1102**	B102WUV
821	RYK821Y	**893**	A893SYE	**963**	A963SYE	**1032**	A632THV	**1103**	B103WUV
822	RYK822Y	**894**c	A894SYE	**964**	A964SYE	**1033**	A633THV	**1104**	B104WUV
823	A823SUL	**895**	A895SYE	**965**u	A965SYE	**1034**	A634THV	**1105**	B105WUV
824	A824SUL	**896**k	A896SYE	**966**	A966SYE	**1035**	A635THV	**1106**	B106WUV
825	A825SUL	**897**	A897SYE	**967**	A967SYE	**1036**	A636THV	**1107**	B107WUV
826	A826SUL	**898**	A898SYE	**968**	A968SYE	**1037**	A637THV	**1108**	B108WUV
827	A827SUL	**899**ku	A899SYE	**969**	A969SYE	**1038**	A638THV	**1109**	B109WUV
828	A828SUL	**901**	A901SYE	**970**	A970SYE	**1040**	A640THV	**1110**	B110WUV
829	A829SUL	**902**u	A902SYE	**971**ku	A971SYE	**1041**	A641THV	**1111**	B111WUV
830	A830SUL	**903**k	A903SYE	**972**	A972SYE	**1042**	A642THV	**1112**	B112WUV
831	A831SUL	**904**k	A904SYE	**973**	A973SYE	**1043**	A643THV	**1113**	B113WUV
832	A832SUL	**905**u	A905SYE	**974**	A974SYE	**1044**	A644THV	**1114**	B114WUV
833	A833SUL	**906**	A906SYE	**975**	A975SYE	**1045**	A645THV	**1115**	B115WUV
834	A834SUL	**907**	A907SYE	**976**	A976SYE	**1046**	A646THV	**1116**	B116WUV
835	A835SUL	**908**	A908SYE	**977**	A977SYE	**1047**	A647THV	**1117**	B117WUV
836	A836SUL	**909**	A909SYE	**978**	A978SYE	**1048**	A648THV	**1118**	B118WUV
837	A837SUL	**910**k	A910SYE	**979**	A979SYE	**1049**	A649THV	**1119**	B119WUV
838	A838SUL	**911**ku	A911SYE	**980**	A980SYE	**1050**ku	A650THV	**1120**	B120WUV
839	A839SUL	**912**k	A912SYE	**981**	A981SYE	**1051**	A651THV	**1121**	B121WUV
840	A840SUL	**913**	A913SYE	**982**	A982SYE	**1052**	A652THV	**1122**	B122WUV
841	A841SUL	**914**	A914SYE	**983**	A983SYE	**1053**c	A653THV	**1123**	B123WUV
842	A842SUL	**915**	A915SYE	**984**	A984SYE	**1054**	A654THV	**1124**	B124WUV
843	A843SUL	**916**	A916SYE	**985**	A985SYE	**1055**	A655THV	**1125**	B125WUV
844	A844SUL	**917**	A917SYE	**986**	A986SYE	**1056**	A56THX	**1126**b	WDA1T
845	A845SUL	**918**	A918SYE	**987**	A987SYE	**1057**	A57THX	**1127**b	WDA2T
846	A846SUL	**919**	A919SYE	**988**	A988SYE	**1058**	A58THX	**1128**b	486CLT
847	A847SUL	**920**	A920SYE	**989**	A989SYE	**1059**	A59THX	**1129**b	WDA4T
848	A848SUL	**921**u	A921SYE	**990**	A990SYE	**1060**	A60THX	**1130**b	WDA5T
849	A849SUL	**922**k	A922SYE	**991**	A991SYE	**1061**	A61THX		
850	A850SUL	**923**	A923SYE	**992**	A992SYE	**1062**	A62THX		

b High-back seating c City of London k Westlink o Open top s Single door conversion u Unlicensed
w Withdrawn

Named vehicles: T 512 *Phoenix*, T 803 *Albatross*, T 1127 *Illustrious*, T 1128 *The Ranger*, T 1129 *Harrier*

Previous owners: T 1126-1130 acquired from West Midlands PTE in 1984

L

Chassis Leyland Olympian ONTL11/1R (L 1) or ONLXB/1R (L 2, 3) or ONLXB/1RH (L 4-263) or ONCL10/1RZ (L 292-306) or ON2R50C13Z4 (L 307-354)
Engine Leyland TL11 11-litre rated at 137kW at 1850rpm (L 1) or Gardner 6LXB 10.45-litre rated at 127kW at 1850rpm (L 2-263) or Cummins LT10-B180 10-litre rated at 134kW at 1850rpm (L 292-354)
Bodywork Eastern Coach Works (1-263) or Leyland (L 292-314) or Alexander 'RH' (L 315-354)
Capacity H47/28D+16 (1-3), H42/26D+20 (4-263), H47/31F+17 (292-311), H43/29F+17 (312-314), H43/25D+15 (315-354)
Built 1984-1992
Dimensions 9563mm x 2502mm x 4331mm (L 315-354 are 9600mm long)
Number Built 354 **Number in Stock** 326 **Number Scheduled for Service** 290 (including 6 express)

1	A101SYE	**67**	C67CHM	**133**	D133FYM	**199**	D199FYM	**293**	G293UYK
2	A102SYE	**68**	C68CHM	**134**	D134FYM	**200**	D200FYM	**294**	G294UYK
3	A103SYE	**69**	C69CHM	**135**	D135FYM	**201**	D201FYM	**295**	G295UYK
4	C804BYY	**70**	C70CHM	**136**c	D136FYM	**202**	D202FYM	**296**	G296UYK
5	C805BYY	**71**	C71CHM	**137**	D137FYM	**203**	D203FYM	**297**	G297UYK
6	C806BYY	**72**	C72CHM	**138**	D138FYM	**204**	D204FYM	**298**	G298UYK
7	C807BYY	**73**	C73CHM	**139**	D139FYM	**205**	D205FYM	**299**	G299UYK
8	WLT807	**74**	C74CHM	**140**	D140FYM	**206**	D206FYM	**300**	G300UYK
9	C809BYY	**75**	C75CHM	**141**	D141FYM	**207**	D207FYM	**301**	G301UYK
10	C810BYY	**76**	C76CHM	**142**	D142FYM	**208**	D208FYM	**302**	G302UYK
11	C811BYY	**77**	C77CHM	**145**	D143FYM	**209**	D209FYM	**303**	G303UYK
12	C812BYY	**78**	C78CHM	**144**	D144FYM	**210**	D210FYM	**304**	G304UYK
13	VLT13	**79**	C79CHM	**145**	D145FYM	**211**	D211FYM	**305**	G305UYK
14	C814BYY	**80**	C80CHM	**146**	D146FYM	**212**	D212FYM	**306**	G306UYK
15	C815BYY	**81**	C81CHM	**147**	D147FYM	**213**	D213FYM	**307**	G307UYK
16	WLT916	**82**	C82CHM	**148**	D148FYM	**214**	D214FYM	**308**	G308UYK
17	C817BYY	**83**	C83CHM	**149**	D149FYM	**215**	815DYE	**309**	G309UYK
18	C818BYY	**84**	C84CHM	**150**	D150FYM	**216**	D216FYM	**310**	G310UYK
19	C819BYY	**85**	C85CHM	**151**	WLT851	**217**	217CLT	**311**	G311UYK
20	C820BYY	**86**	C86CHM	**152**	D152FYM	**218**	D218FYM	**312**b	G312UYK
21	C21CHM	**87**	C87CHM	**153**	D153FYM	**219**	519CLT	**313**b	G313UYK
22	C22CHM	**88**	C88CHM	**154**	WLT554	**220**	D220FYM	**314**b	G314UYK
23	C23CHM	**89**	C89CHM	**155**	D155FYM	**221**	D221FYM	**315**	J315BSH
24	C24CHM	**90**	C90CHM	**156**	656DYE	**222**	D222FYM	**316**	J316BSH
25	C25CHM	**91**	C91CHM	**157**	D157FYM	**223**	D223FYM	**317**	J317BSH
26	C26CHM	**92**	C92CHM	**158**	D158FYM	**224**	D224FYM	**318**	J318BSH
27	VLT27	**93**	C93CHM	**159**	D159FYM	**225**	D225FYM	**319**	J319BSH
28	C28CHM	**94**	C94CHM	**160**	D160FYM	**226**	D226FYM	**320**	J320BSH
29	C29CHM	**95**	VLT29	**161**	D161FYM	**227**	D227FYM	**321**	J321BSH
30	C30CHM	**96**	C96CHM	**162**	D162FYM	**228**	D228FYM	**322**	J322BSH
31	C31CHM	**97**	C97CHM	**163**	D163FYM	**229**	D229FYM	**323**	J323BSH
32	C32CHM	**98**	C98CHM	**164**	D164FYM	**230**	D230FYM	**324**	J324BSH
33	330CLT	**99**	C99CHM	**165**	D165FYM	**231**	D231FYM	**325**	J325BSH
34	C34CHM	**100**	C100CHM	**166**b	D166FYM	**232**	D232FYM	**326**	J326BSH
35	C35CHM	**101**	C101CHM	**167**b	D167FYM	**233**	D233FYM	**327**	J327BSH
36	C36CHM	**102**	C102CHM	**168**b	D168FYM	**234**	D234FYM	**328**	J328BSH
37	C37CHM	**103**	C103CHM	**169**b	D169FYM	**235**	D235FYM	**329**	J329BSH
38	C38CHM	**104**	C104CHM	**170**b	7CLT	**236**	D236FYM	**330**	J330BSH
39	C39CHM	**105**	C105CHM	**171**b	D171FYM	**237**	D237FYM	**331**	J331BSH
40	C40CHM	**106**	C106CHM	**172**	WLT372	**238**	D238FYM	**332**	J332BSH
41	C41CHM	**107**	C107CHM	**173**	VLT173	**239**	D239FYM	**333**	J433BSH
42	C42CHM	**108**	C108CHM	**174**	D174FYM	**240**	D240FYM	**334**	J334BSH
43	C43CHM	**109**	C109CHM	**175**	D175FYM	**241**	D241FYM	**335**	J335BSH
44	C44CHM	**110**	C110CHM	**176**	D176FYM	**242**	D242FYM	**336**	J336BSH
45	C45CHM	**111**	C111CHM	**177**	D177FYM	**243**	D243FYM	**337**	J337BSH
46	C46CHM	**112**	C112CHM	**178**	D178FYM	**244**	VLT244	**338**	J338BSH
47	VLT47	**113**	C113CHM	**179**	D179FYM	**245**	D245FYM	**339**	J339BSH
48	C48CHM	**114**	C114CHM	**180**	480CLT	**246**	D246FYM	**340**	J340BSH
49	C49CHM	**115**	C115CHM	**181**	D181FYM	**247**	D247FYM	**341**	J341BSH
50	C50CHM	**116**	C116CHM	**182**	D182FYM	**248**	D248FYM	**342**	J342BSH
51	C51CHM	**117**	C117CHM	**183**	D183FYM	**249**	D249FYM	**343**	J343BSH
52	C52CHM	**118**	C118CHM	**184**	D184FYM	**250**	D250FYM	**344**	J344BSH
53	C53CHM	**119**	C119CHM	**185**	D185FYM	**251**	D251FYM	**345**	J345BSH
54	C54CHM	**120**	C120CHM	**186**	D186FYM	**252**	D252FYM	**346**	J346BSH
55	C55CHM	**121**	C121CHM	**187**	D187FYM	**253**	D253FYM	**347**	J347BSH
56	C56CHM	**122**	C122CHM	**188**	D188FYM	**254**	D254FYM	**348**	J348BSH
57	C57CHM	**123**	D123FYM	**189**	D189FYM	**255**	D255FYM	**349**	J349BSH
58	C58CHM	**124**	D124FYM	**190**	319CLT	**256**	D256FYM	**350**	J350BSH
59	C59CHM	**125**	D125FYM	**191**	D191FYM	**257**	D257FYM	**351**	J351BSH
60	C60CHM	**126**	D126FYM	**192**	D192FYM	**258**	D258FYM	**352**	J352BSH
61	C61CHM	**127**	D127FYM	**193**	D193FYM	**259**	D259FYM	**353**	J353BSH
62	C62CHM	**128**	D128FYM	**194**	D194FYM	**260**b	VLT20	**354**	J354BSH
63	C63CHM	**129**	D129FYM	**195**	D195FYM	**261**b	2CLT		
64	C64CHM	**130**	D130FYM	**196**	D196FYM	**262**b	VLT14		
65	C65CHM	**131**	D131FYM	**197**	D197FYM	**263**b	VLT9		
66	C66CHM	**132**	D132FYM	**198**	D198FYM	**292**	G292UYK		

b High-back seating   c Lewisham Tramways livery
Named vehicles: L 93 *Hawk*, L 95 *Hunter*, L 260 *Renown*, L 261 *Buccaneer*, L 262 *Invincible*, L 263 *Conqueror*

V

Chassis Volvo Ailsa B55C/1 MkIII
Engine Volvo TD70H 6.7-litre rated at 144kW at 2200rpm
Bodywork Alexander 'RV' H47/31D+8
Built 1984
Dimensions 9779mm x 2502mm x 4420mm
Number Built 3
Number in Stock 2

1	A101SUU	**2**	A102SUU

VC

Chassis Volvo Citybus B10M-50
Engine Volvo TDH101GB 9.6-litre rated at 165kW at 2200rpm
Bodywork Northern Counties H45/35D+13 (VC 1-6), H47/35D+13 (VC 7-39)
Built 1989-1991
Dimensions 9830mm x 2502mm x 4420mm
Number Built and in Stock 39
Number Scheduled for Service 34

1b	101CLT	**9**	G109NGN	**17**	G117NGN	**25**	125CLT	**33**	G133PGK
2b	G102NGN	**10**	G110NGN	**18**	WLT818	**26**	G126NGN	**34**	G134PGK
3b	WLT803	**11**	WLT311	**19**	619DYE	**27**	G127NGN	**35**	G135PGK
4	WLT474	**12**	G112NGN	**20**	G120NGN	**28**	G128PGK	**36**	836DYE
5	G105NGN	**13**	G113NGN	**21**	621DYE	**29**	229CLT	**37**	WLT837
6	VLT60	**14**	614DYE	**22**	G122NGN	**30**	G130PGK	**38**	G138PGK
7	G107NGN	**15**	G115NGN	**23**	23CLT	**31**	G131PGK	**39**	839DYE
8	G108NGN	**16**	G116NGN	**24**	G124NGN	**32**	G132PGK		

b High-back seating

S

Chassis Scania N112DRB (S1-9), N113DRB (S10-71)
Engine Scania DS11-25 11-litre rated at 189kW at 2000rpm
Bodywork Alexander 'RH' (S 1-29) or Northern Counties (S 30-71)
Capacity H47/33F+18 (S 1-9, 30/1), H47/31F+20 (S 10-29), H41/25D+20 (S 32-71)
Built 1989-1992
Dimensions 9700mm x 2502mm x 4496mm (S 1-29), 9720mm x 2502mm x 4400mm (S 30-71)
Number Built and in Stock 71
Number Scheduled for Service 70

1	F421GWG	**16**x	J816HMC	**31**d	J231XKY	**46**	K846LMK	**61**	K861LMK
2	F422GWG	**17**x	J817HMC	**32**d	J132HMT	**47**	K847LMK	**62**	K862LMK
3	F423GWG	**18**a	J818HMC	**33**d	J133HMT	**48**	K848LMK	**63**	K863LMK
4	F424GWG	**19**x	J819HMC	**34**d	J134HMT	**49**	K849LMK	**64**	K864LMK
5	F425GWG	**20**x	J820HMC	**35**d	J135HMT	**50**	K850LMK	**65**	K865LMK
6	F426GWG	**21**d	J821HMC	**36**d	J136HMT	**51**	K851LMK	**66**	K866LMK
7	F427GWG	**22**d	J822HMC	**37**d	J137HMT	**52**	K852LMK	**67**	K867LMK
8	F428GWG	**23**d	J823HMC	**38**d	J138HMT	**53**	K853LMK	**68**	K868LMK
9	F429GWG	**24**d	J824HMC	**39**d	J139HMT	**54**	K854LMK	**69**	K869LMK
10	J810HMC	**25**d	J825HMC	**40**d	J140HMT	**55**	K855LMK	**70**	K870LMK
11x	J811HMC	**26**d	J826HMC	**41**	J141HMT	**56**	K856LMK	**71**	K871LMK
12	J812HMC	**27**d	J827HMC	**42**	J142HMT	**57**	K857LMK		
13x	J813HMC	**28**d	J828HMC	**43**	J143HMT	**58**	K858LMK		
14x	J814HMC	**29**d	J829HMC	**44**	J144HMT	**59**	K859LMK		
15x	J815HMC	**30**d	J230XKY	**45**	J145HMT	**60**	K860LMK		

d Docklands Express livery x Route X43 livery

SP

Chassis DAF DB250WB505
Engine DAF RS200 8.65-litre rated at 200kW at 2300rpm
Bodywork Optare H44/27F+8 (SP2: H44/23D+14)
Built 1992-1993
Dimensions 10128mm x 2502mm x 4318mm
Number Built and in Stock 25
Number Scheduled for Service 24

1	K301FYG	**6**	K306FYG	**11**	K311FYG	**16**	K316FYG	**21**	K321FYG
2	K302FYG	**7**	K307FYG	**12**	K312FYG	**17**	K317FYG	**22**	K322FYG
3	K303FYG	**8**	K308FYG	**13**	K313FYG	**18**	18CLT	**23**	K323FYG
4	K304FYG	**9**	K309FYG	**14**	K314FYG	**19**	19CLT	**24**	K324FYG
5	K305FYG	**10**	K310FYG	**15**	K315FYG	**20**	20CLT	**25**	K325FYG

SINGLE DECKERS AND MINIBUSES
Listed in alphabetical order

A

Chassis Dodge S56
Engine Perkins 4.05-litre rated at 69kW at 3600 rpm
Bodywork Rootes B19F
Built 1983
Dimensions 5892mm x 2184mm x 2718mm
Number Built 2
Number in Stock 1

1	NYN1Y	Staff bus

BL

Chassis Bristol LH6L
Engine Leyland E0401 6.54-litre developing 125bhp at 2400rpm
Bodywork Eastern Coach Works B39F (BL 36, 81: DP40F)
Built 1976-1977
Dimensions 9182mm x 2324mm x 3054mm
Number Built 95
Number in Stock 24

1t	KJD401P	**31**tu	KJD431P	**49**t	OJD49R	**78**t	OJD78R	**84**tu	OJD84R
2t	KJD402P	**33**tu	KJD433P	**57**t	OJD57R	**79**w	OJD79R	**85**t	OJD85R
4t	KJD404P	**34**t	KJD434P	**65**t	OJD65R	**80**tu	OJD80R	**86**t	OJD86R
9w	KJD409P	**35**t	KJD435P	**66**w	OJD66R	**81**t	OJD81R	**91**t	OJD91R
28t	KJD428P	**36**t	KJD436P	**69**t	OJD69R	**83**w	OJD83R		

t Trainer u Unlicensed

CV

Chassis CVE Omni
Engine Land Rover 2.5-litre turbocharged rated at 63kW at 4000rpm
Bodywork City Vehicle Engineering B20FL (CV 5-7: B23FL)
Built 1989-1990
Dimensions 6625mm x 2390mm x 2442mm
Number Built 7 (including acquisitions)
Number in Stock 6
Number Scheduled for Service 4

1k	F265WDC	**3**k	F267WDC	**5**	A2LBR	**6**	A3LBR	**7**	A4LBR
2	F266WDC								

k Westlink livery
CV 1-3 are owned by the London Borough of Hounslow and CV 5-7 by the London Borough of Richmond-upon-Thames
Named vehicle: CV 1 *County of Middlesex*
Previous owners: CV 5-7 acquired from C&M, Aintree in 1992

DA

Chassis DAF SB220LC550
Engine DAF LC1160 11.6-litre rated at 161kW at 2000rpm
Bodywork Optare DP49F+24 (DA 1), B49F+24 (DA 2-9), DP36D+39 (DA 10), B40D+31 (DA 11-35)
Built 1989-1993
Dimensions 11800mm x 2502mm x 3140mm
Number Built 35 (including acquisition)
Number in Stock 35
Number Scheduled for Service 25

1	F802NGY	**8**k	G936MYG	**15**	J715CYG	**22**	J722CYG	**29**	J729CYG
2k	A5LBR	**9**k	G937MYG	**16**	J716CYG	**23**	J723CYG	**30**	K630HWX
3k	G931MYG	**10**	G684KNW	**17**	J717CYG	**24**	J724CYG	**31**	K631HWX
4k	G932MYG	**11**	J711CYG	**18**	J718CYG	**25**	J725CYG	**32**	K632HWX
5k	G933MYG	**12**	J712CYG	**19**	J719CYG	**26**	J726CYG	**33**	K633HWX
6k	G934MYG	**13**	J713CYG	**20**	J720CYG	**27**	J727CYG	**34**	K634HWX
7k	G935MYG	**14**	J714CYG	**21**	J721CYG	**28**	J728CYG	**35**	K635HWX

k Westlink livery (all others are in East London livery)
Previous owners: DA 10 acquired from Optare, Leeds (demonstrator) in 1991

DR

Chassis Dennis Dart 8.5SDL3003 (DR 1-52), 8.5SDL3010 (DR 53-141), 8.5SDL3015 (DR 142-153)
Engine Cummins 6BT5.9 5.88-litre turbocharged rated at 119kW at 2500rpm
Bodywork Reeve Burgess (DR 1-19) or Plaxton Pointer (DR 20-153)
Capacity B28F+13 (DR 1-55, 81-98, 142-153) or B24F+21 (DR 56-80, 99-141)
Built 1991-1993
Dimensions 8453mm x 2293mm x 2865mm
Number Built and in Stock 153
Number Scheduled for Service 134

1	H101THE	**32**s	WLT352	**63**	J363GKH	**94**	J394GKH	**125**	J125DUV
2	H102THE	**33**s	H533XGK	**64**	J364GKH	**95**	J395GKH	**126**	J126DUV
3	H103THE	**34**s	H534XGK	**65**	J365GKH	**96**	J396GKH	**127**	J127DUV
4	H104THE	**35**s	H835XGK	**66**	J366GKH	**97**	J397GKH	**128**	J128DUV
5	H105THE	**36**s	H536XGK	**67**	J367GKH	**98**	J398GKH	**129**	J129DUV
6	H106THE	**37**s	H537XGK	**68**	J368GKH	**99**	J599DUV	**130**	J130DUV
7	H107THE	**38**s	H538XGK	**69**	J369GKH	**100**	J610DUV	**131**	J131DUV
8	H108THE	**39**s	H539XGK	**70**	J370GKH	**101**	J101DUV	**132**	J132DUV
9	H109THE	**40**s	H540XGK	**71**	J371GKH	**102**	J102DUV	**133**	J133DUV
10	H110THE	**41**s	H541XGK	**72**	J372GKH	**103**	J103DUV	**134**	J134DUV
11	H611TKU	**42**s	H542XGK	**73**	J373GKH	**104**	J104DUV	**135**	J135DUV
12	H112THE	**43**s	H543XGK	**74**	J374GKH	**105**	J105DUV	**136**	J136DUV
13	H113THE	**44**s	H544XGK	**75**	J375GKH	**106**	J106DUV	**137**	J137DUV
14	H114THE	**45**s	H545XGK	**76**	J376GKH	**107**	J107DUV	**138**	J138DUV
15	H115THE	**46**s	46CLT	**77**	J377GKH	**108**	J108DUV	**139**	J139DUV
16	H116THE	**47**s	H547XGK	**78**	J378GKH	**109**	J109DUV	**140**	J140DUV
17	H117THE	**48**s	H548XGK	**79**	J379GKH	**110**	J110DUV	**141**	J141DUV
18	H118THE	**49**s	H549XGK	**80**	J380GKH	**111**	J611DUV	**142**	K242PAG
19	H119THE	**50**s	H550XGK	**81**	J381GKH	**112**	J112DUV	**143**	K243PAG
20	H120THE	**51**s	H551XGK	**82**	J382GKH	**113**	J113DUV	**144**	K244PAG
21	H621TKU	**52**s	H552XGK	**83**	J383GKH	**114**	J114DUV	**145**	K245PAG
22	H122THE	**53**	J653XHL	**84**	J384GKH	**115**	J115DUV	**146**	K246PAG
23	H123THE	**54**	J654XHL	**85**	J385GKH	**116**	J116DUV	**147**	K247PAG
24	H124THE	**55**	J655XHL	**86**	J386GKH	**117**	J117DUV	**148**	K248PAG
25	H125THE	**56**	J156GAT	**87**	J387GKH	**118**	J118DUV	**149**s	K149LGO
26	H126THE	**57**	J157GAT	**88**	J388GKH	**119**	J119DUV	**150**s	K150LGO
27	H127THE	**58**	J158GAT	**89**	J389GKH	**120**	J120DUV	**151**s	K151LGO
28	H128THE	**59**	J159GAT	**90**	J390GKH	**121**	J121DUV	**152**s	K152LGO
29	H129THE	**60**	J160GAT	**91**	J391GKH	**122**	J122DUV	**153**s	K153LGO
30	H130THE	**61**	J161GAT	**92**	J392GKH	**123**	J123DUV		
31	H131THE	**62**	J362GKH	**93**	J393GKH	**124**	J124DUV		

s Streetline livery

DRL

Chassis Dennis Dart 9SDL3011 (DRL 1-16), 9SDL3016 (DRL 17-73), 9SDL3024 (DRL 74-138, 147-158) 9SDL3034 (DRL 139-46, 159-164)
Engine Cummins 6BT5.9 5.88-litre turbocharged rated at 119kW at 2500rpm
Bodywork Plaxton Pointer B34F+16 (DRL 1-73, 109-158), B32F+15 (DRL 74-95), B28F+23 (DRL 96-108, 159-164)
Built 1991-1993
Dimensions 8988mm x 2293mm x 2865mm
Number Built and On Order 164
Number Scheduled for Service 77

1	J601HXL	**17**	K817NKH	**33**	K433OKH	**49**	K549ORH	**65**	K865LGN
2	J602HXL	**18**	K818NKH	**34**	K434OKH	**50**	K550ORH	**66**	K866LGN
3	J603HXL	**19**	K819NKH	**35**	K435OKH	**51**	K551ORH	**67**	K867LGN
4	J604HXL	**20**	K820NKH	**36**	K436OKH	**52**	K552ORH	**68**	K868LGN
5	J605HXL	**21**	K821NKH	**37**	K437OKH	**53**	K853LGN	**69**	K869LGN
6	J606HXL	**22**	K822NKH	**38**	K538ORH	**54**	K854LGN	**70**	K870LGN
7	J607HXL	**23**	K823NKH	**39**	K539ORH	**55**	K855LGN	**71**	K871LGN
8	J608HXL	**24**	K824NKH	**40**	K540ORH	**56**	K856LGN	**72**	K872LGN
9	J609HXL	**25**	K825NKH	**41**	K541ORH	**57**	K857LGN	**73**	K873LGN
10	J610HXL	**26**	K826NKH	**42**	K542ORH	**58**	K858LGN	**74**	K574MGT
11	J611HXL	**27**	K827NKH	**43**	K543ORH	**59**	K859LGN	**75**	K575MGT
12	J612HXL	**28**	K828NKH	**44**	K544ORH	**60**	K860LGN	**76**	K576MGT
13	J613HXL	**29**	K429OKH	**45**	K545ORH	**61**	K861LGN	**77**	K577MGT
14	J614HXL	**30**	K430OKH	**46**	K546ORH	**62**	K862LGN	**78**	K578MGT
15	J615HXL	**31**	K431OKH	**47**	K547ORH	**63**	K863LGN	**79**	K579MGT
16	J616HXL	**32**	K432OKH	**48**	K548ORH	**64**	K864LGN	**80**	K580MGT

Named vehicles: DRL 1 *Del Boy*, DRL 2 *Rodney*, DRL 3 *Uncle Albert*, DRL 4 *Cassandra*

DRL

81	K581MGT	**98**	K98SAG	**115**	K115SRH	**132**	K132SRH	**149**	
82	K582MGT	**99**	K199SAG	**116**	K116SRH	**133**	K133SRH	**150**	
83	K583MGT	**100**	K210SAG	**117**	K117SRH	**134**	K134SRH	**151**	
84	K584MGT	**101**	K101SAG	**118**	K118SRH	**135**	K135SRH	**152**	
85	K585MGT	**102**	K102SAG	**119**	K119SRH	**136**		**153**	
86	K586MGT	**103**	K103SAG	**120**	K120SRH	**137**		**154**	
87	K587MGT	**104**	K104SAG	**121**	K121SRH	**138**		**155**	
88	K588MGT	**105**	K105SAG	**122**	K122SRH	**139**		**156**	
89	K589MGT	**106**	K106SAG	**123**	K123SRH	**140**		**157**	
90	K590MGT	**107**	K107SAG	**124**	K124SRH	**141**		**158**	
91	K591MGT	**108**	K108SAG	**125**	K125SRH	**142**		**159**	
92	K592MGT	**109**	K109SRH	**126**	K126SRH	**143**		**160**	
93	K593MGT	**110**	K110SRH	**127**	K127SRH	**144**		**161**	
94	K594MGT	**111**	K211SRH	**128**	K128SRH	**145**		**162**	
95	K595MGT	**112**	K112SRH	**129**	K129SRH	**146**		**163**	
96	K96SAG	**113**	K113SRH	**130**	K130SRH	**147**		**164**	
97	K97SAG	**114**	K114SRH	**131**	K131SRH	**148**			

DT

Chassis Dennis Dart 8.5SDL3003
Engine Cummins 6BT5.9 5.88-litre turbocharged rated at 119kW at 2500rpm
Bodywork Duple (DT 1-27, 168) or Carlyle (DT 28-167) B28F+13 (DT 28, 30/1, 55: DP28F+13)
Built 1990-1991
Dimensions 8475mm x 2286mm x 2780mm
Number Built and in Stock 168 (including acquisition)
Number Scheduled for Service 150

1	G501VYE	**35**	G35TGW	**69**	H469UGO	**103**	H103MOB	**137**	H137MOB
2	G502VYE	**36**	G36TGW	**70**	H470UGO	**104**	H104MOB	**138**	H138MOB
3	G503VYE	**37**	G37TGW	**71**	H71MOB	**105**	H105MOB	**139**	H139MOB
4	G504VYE	**38**	G38TGW	**72**	H72MOB	**106**	H106MOB	**140**	H140MOB
5	G505VYE	**39**	G39TGW	**73**	H73MOB	**107**	H107MOB	**141**	H141MOB
6	G506VYE	**40**	G40TGW	**74**	H74MOB	**108**	H108MOB	**142**	H142MOB
7	G507VYE	**41**	G41TGW	**75**	H575MOC	**109**	H109MOB	**143**	H143MOB
8	G508VYE	**42**	G42TGW	**76**	H76MOB	**110**	H110MOB	**144**	H144MOB
9	G509VYE	**43**	G43TGW	**77**	H577MOC	**111**	H611MOM	**145**	H145MOB
10	G510VYE	**44**	G44TGW	**78**	H78MOB	**112**	H112MOB	**146**	H146MOB
11	G511VYE	**45**	G45TGW	**79**	H79MOB	**113**	H113MOB	**147**	H147MOB
12	G512VYE	**46**	G46TGW	**80**	H880LOX	**114**	H114MOB	**148**	H148MOB
13	G513VYE	**47**	G47TGW	**81**	H81MOB	**115**	H115MOB	**149**	H149MOB
14	G514VYE	**48**	G48TGW	**82**	H82MOB	**116**	H116MOB	**150**	H150MOB
15	G515VYE	**49**	G49TGW	**83**	H83MOB	**117**	H117MOB	**151**	H151MOB
16	G516VYE	**50**	G50TGW	**84**	H84MOB	**118**	H118MOB	**152**	H152MOB
17	G517VYE	**51**	G51TGW	**85**	H85MOB	**119**	H119MOB	**153**	H153MOB
18	G518VYE	**52**	G52TGW	**86**	H86MOB	**120**	H120MOB	**154**	H154MOB
19	G519VYE	**53**	G53TGW	**87**	H87MOB	**121**	H621MOM	**155**	H155MOB
20	G520VYE	**54**	G54TGW	**88**	H588MOC	**122**	H122MOB	**156**	H156MOB
21	G521VYE	**55**	WLT575	**89**	H89MOB	**123**	H123MOB	**157**	H157NON
22	G522VYE	**56**	G56TGW	**90**	H890LOX	**124**	H124MOB	**158**	H158NON
23	G523VYE	**57**	G57TGW	**91**	H91MOB	**125**	H125MOB	**159**	H159NON
24	G524VYE	**58**	H458UGO	**92**	H92MOB	**126**	H126MOB	**160**	H160NON
25	G525VYE	**59**	H459UGO	**93**	H93MOB	**127**	H127MOB	**161**	H161NON
26	G526VYE	**60**	H460UGO	**94**	H94MOB	**128**	H128MOB	**162**	H162NON
27	G527VYE	**61**	H461UGO	**95**	H95MOB	**129**	H129MOB	**163**	H163NON
28	49CLT	**62**	H462UGO	**96**	H96MOB	**130**	H130MOB	**164**	H264NON
29	G29TGW	**63**	H463UGO	**97**	H97MOB	**131**	H131MOB	**165**	H165NON
30	G30TGW	**64**	H464UGO	**98**	H98MOB	**132**	H132MOB	**166**	H166NON
31	G31TGW	**65**	H465UGO	**99**	H99MOB	**133**	H133MOB	**167**	H167NON
32	VLT240	**66**	H466UGO	**100**	H620MOM	**134**	H134MOB	**168**	500CLT
33	G33TGW	**67**	H467UGO	**101**	H101MOB	**135**	H135MOB		
34	G34TGW	**68**	H468UGO	**102**	H102MOB	**136**	H136MOB		

Named vehicle: DT 28 *Pride of Carlyle*

Previous owner: DT 168 Carlyle, Birmingham (demonstrator) in 1990

DW

Chassis Dennis Dart 8.5SDL3003 (DW 1-91, 100), 8.5SDL3010 (DW 92-9, 101-114), 8.5SDL3015 (DW 115-25/7-70), 8.5SDL3018 (DW 126)
Engine Cummins 6BT5.9 5.88-litre turbocharged rated at 119kW at 2500rpm
Bodywork Wright 'Handybus' B30F+15 (DW1-14, 44-58), B26F+20 (DW15-43, 72-126/69/70), B28F+16 (DW 59-65, 71), B29F+16 (DW 66-70, 127-168)
Built 1990-1993
Dimensions 8485mm x 2300mm x 2700mm
Number Built and in Stock 170
Number Scheduled for Service 149

1	JDZ2301	**35**	JDZ2335	**69**	H369XGC	**103**	KDZ5103	**137**	NDZ3137
2	JDZ2302	**36**	JDZ2336	**70**	H370XGC	**104**	KDZ5104	**138**	NDZ3138
3	JDZ2303	**37**	JDZ2337	**71**	JDZ2371	**105**	KDZ5105	**139**	NDZ3139
4	JDZ2304	**38**	JDZ2338	**72**	JDZ2372	**106**	KDZ5106	**140**	NDZ3140
5	JDZ2305	**39**	JDZ2339	**73**	JDZ2373	**107**	KDZ5107	**141**	NDZ3141
6	JDZ2306	**40**	JDZ2340	**74**	JDZ2374	**108**	KDZ5108	**142**	NDZ3142
7	JDZ2307	**41**	JDZ2341	**75**	JDZ2375	**109**	KDZ5109	**143**	NDZ3143
8	JDZ2308	**42**	JDZ2342	**76**	JDZ2376	**110**	KDZ5110	**144**	NDZ3144
9	JDZ2309	**43**	JDZ2343	**77**	JDZ2377	**111**	KDZ5111	**145**	NDZ3145
10	JDZ2310	**44**s	JDZ2344	**78**	JDZ2378	**112**	KDZ5112	**146**	NDZ3146
11	JDZ2311	**45**s	545CLT	**79**	JDZ2379	**113**	LDZ9113	**147**	NDZ3147
12	JDZ2312	**46**s	WLT346	**80**	JDZ2380	**114**	LDZ9114	**148**	NDZ3148
13	JDZ2313	**47**s	JDZ2347	**81**	JDZ2381	**115**	LDZ9115	**149**	NDZ3149
14	JDZ2314	**48**s	WLT548	**82**	JDZ2382	**116**	LDZ9116	**150**	NDZ3150
15	JDZ2315	**49**s	JDZ2349	**83**	JDZ2383	**117**	LDZ9117	**151**	NDZ3151
16	JDZ2316	**50**s	JDZ2350	**84**	JDZ2384	**118**	LDZ9118	**152**	NDZ3152
17	JDZ2317	**51**s	JDZ2351	**85**	JDZ2385	**119**	LDZ9119	**153**	NDZ3153
18	JDZ2318	**52**	352CLT	**86**	JDZ2386	**120**	LDZ9120	**154**	NDZ3154
19	JDZ2319	**53**s	JDZ2353	**87**	JDZ2387	**121**	LDZ9121	**155**	NDZ3155
20	JDZ2320	**54**s	JDZ2354	**88**	JDZ2388	**122**	LDZ9122	**156**	NDZ3156
21	JDZ2321	**55**	JDZ2355	**89**	JDZ2389	**123**	LDZ9123	**157**	NDZ3157
22	JDZ2322	**56**s	JDZ2356	**90**	JDZ2390	**124**	LDZ9124	**158**	NDZ3158
23	JDZ2323	**57**s	DZ2357	**91**	JDZ2391	**125**	LDZ9125	**159**	NDZ3159
24	JDZ2324	**58**	JDZ2358	**92**	JDZ2392	**126**	LDZ9126	**160**	NDZ3160
25	JDZ2325	**59**	JDZ2359	**93**	JDZ2393	**127**s	K127LGO	**161**	NDZ3161
26	JDZ2326	**60**	JDZ2360	**94**	JDZ2394	**128**s	K128LGO	**162**	NDZ3162
27	JDZ2327	**61**	JDZ2361	**95**	JDZ2395	**129**s	K129LGO	**163**	NDZ3163
28	JDZ2328	**62**	JDZ2362	**96**	JDZ2396	**130**s	K130LGO	**164**	NDZ3164
29	JDZ2329	**63**	JDZ2363	**97**	JDZ2397	**131**s	K131LGO	**165**	NDZ3165
30	JDZ2330	**64**	JDZ2364	**98**	JDZ2398	**132**s	K132LGO	**166**	NDZ3166
31	JDZ2331	**65**	JDZ2365	**99**	JDZ2399	**133**	NDZ3133	**167**	NDZ3167
32	JDZ2332	**66**	166CLT	**100**	JDZ2300	**134**	NDZ3134	**168**	NDZ3168
33	JDZ2333	**67**	H367XGC	**101**	KDZ5101	**135**	NDZ3135	**169**	NDZ3169
34	JDZ2334	**68**	H368XGC	**102**	KDZ5102	**136**	NDZ3136	**170**	NDZ3170

Named vehicles: DW 1 *Andromeda,* DW 2 *Leo,* DW 3 *Pegasus,* DW 4 *Endamus,* DW 5 *Rigel,* DW 6 *Taurus,* DW 7 *Orion,* DW 8 *Nebulus,* DW 9 *Grus,* DW 10 *Aquila,* DW 11 *Regulus,* DW 12 *Aries,* DW 13 *Gemini,* DW 14 *Equulus*

s Streetline livery

Previous owner: DW 100 Wright, Belfast (demonstrator) in 1991

DWL

Chassis Dennis Dart 9SDL3002 (DWL 1-14), 9SDL3016 (DWL 15-26)
Engine Cummins 6BT5.9 5.88-litre turbocharged rated at 119kW at 2500rpm
Bodywork Wright 'Handybus' B35F+17
Built 1990, 1993
Dimensions 9010mm x 2300mm x 2700mm
Number Built and in Stock 26
Number Scheduled for Service 23

1p	JDZ2401	**7**k	JDZ2407	**12**k	JDZ2412	**17**	NDZ3017	**22**	NDZ3022
2p	JDZ2402	**8**k	JDZ2408	**13**k	JDZ2413	**18**	NDZ3018	**23**	NDZ3023
3k	JDZ2403	**9**k	JDZ2409	**14**k	JDZ2414	**19**	NDZ3019	**24**	NDZ3024
4k	JDZ2404	**10**k	JDZ2410	**15**	NDZ3015	**20**	NDZ3020	**25**	NDZ3025
5k	JDZ2405	**11**k	JDZ2411	**16**	NDZ3016	**21**	NDZ3021	**26**	NDZ3026
6k	JDZ2406								

k Westlink livery p Kingston University livery

FM

Chassis Fiat Iveco Daily 49-10
Engine Iveco 8140.27 2.45-litre turbocharged rated at 76kW at 3800rpm
Bodywork Marshall 'C31' B23F
Built 1993
Dimensions 6920mm x 2200mm x 2900mm
Number Built and in Stock 10
Number Scheduled for Service 10

1	K521DFL	**3**	K523DFL	**5**	K525DFL	**7**	K527DFL	**9**	K529FDL
2	K522DFL	**4**	K524DFL	**6**	K526DFL	**8**	K528DFL	**10**	K530DFL

FR

Chassis Fiat Iveco Daily 49-10
Engine Iveco 8140.27 2.45-litre turbocharged rated at 76kW at 3800rpm
Bodywork Reeve Burgess B20FL+4
Built 1990
Dimensions 7115mm x 2320mm x 2642mm
Number Built and in Stock 8
Number Scheduled for Service 7

1	H701YUV	**3**	H703YUV	**5**	H705YUV	**7**	H707YUV	**8**	H708YUV
2	H702YUV	**4**	H704YUV	**6**	H706YUV				

All owned by the London Borough of Hounslow and in white and green livery

FS

Chassis Ford Transit 190 LWB
Engine Ford 2.5-litre rated at 51kW at 4000rpm
Bodywork Carlyle B20F
Built 1985
Dimensions 5928mm x 2140mm x 2731mm
Number Built 29
Number in Stock 1

29 C501HOE

GLS

Sub frames Leyland National 2 NL106L11/2R (GLS 2: NL116AL11/2R)
Engine Gardner 6HLXB 10.45-litre rated at 140kW at 1850rpm
Bodywork Leyland National B24D+48 (GLS 2: DP49F)
Rebuilt 1992
Dimensions 10600mm x 2502mm x 3307mm (GLS 1), 11730mm x 2502mm x 3307mm (GLS 2)
Number rebuilt and in Stock 2 (a further 41 on order)
Number Scheduled for Service 1

1 GUW466W **2** 292CLT

Previous owner: GLS 2 acquired from North Western in 1992

LA

Chassis Dennis Lance 11SDA3101
Engine Cummins 6CT8.3 8.27-litre turbocharged developing 211bhp at 2400rpm
Bodywork Alexander 'PS' B39D+32
Built 1992
Dimensions 11652mm x 2502mm x 2782mm
Number Built and in Stock 16
Number Scheduled for Service 13

1	J101WSC	**5**	J105WSC	**8**	J108WSC	**11**	J411WSC	**14**	J114WSC
2	J102WSC	**6**	J106WSC	**9**	J109WSC	**12**	J112WSC	**15**	J115WSC
3	J103WSC	**7**	J107WSC	**10**	J110WSC	**13**	J113WSC	**16**	J116WSC
4	J104WSC								

LLW

Chassis Dennis Lance SLF
Engine Cummins 6CT8.3 8.27-litre developing 211bhp at 2400rpm
Bodywork Wright 'Pathfinder 320' B35D
Built 1993
Dimensions
Number on Order 38

1	**9**	**17**	**25**	**33**
2	**10**	**18**	**26**	**34**
3	**11**	**19**	**27**	**35**
4	**12**	**20**	**28**	**36**
5	**13**	**21**	**29**	**37**
6	**14**	**22**	**30**	**38**
7	**15**	**23**	**31**	
8	**16**	**24**	**32**	

LN

Chassis Dennis Lance 11SDA3108
Engine Cummins 6CT8.3 8.27-litre turbocharged developing 211bhp at 2400rpm
Bodywork Northern Counties B37D+30
Built 1993
Dimensions 11800mm x 2502mm x 2864mm
Number Built and on Order 31
Number Scheduled for Service 30

1	K301YJA	**8**	K308YJA	**14**	K314YJA	**20**	K320YJA	**26**	K326YJA
2	K302YJA	**9**	K309YJA	**15**	K315YJA	**21**	K321YJA	**27**	K327YJA
3	K303YJA	**10**	K310YJA	**16**	K316YJA	**22**	K322YJA	**28**	K328YJA
4	K304YJA	**11**	K311YJA	**17**	K317YJA	**23**	K323YJA	**29**	K329YJA
5	K305YJA	**12**	K312YJA	**18**	K318YJA	**24**	K324YJA	**30**	K330YJA
6	K306YJA	**13**	K313YJA	**19**	K319YJA	**25**	K325YJA	**31**	K331YJA
7	K307YJA								

Named vehicle: LN 1 *Princess Madden*

LS 7-435

Sub-frames Leyland National 10351A/2R
Engine Leyland 510 8.2-litre turbocharged rated at 119kW at 2000rpm
Bodywork Leyland National B36D+27 (except LS 7, 88, 177, 227/45/59, 395 are DP36F; LS 27, 30, 71/9 are DP24F; LS 35, 97, 123, 411/35 are DP35F; LS 105/21/39, 293, 320, 403 are B21DL)
Built 1976-1979
Dimensions 10395mm x 2502mm x 3315mm
Number Built 437
Number in Stock 56
Number Scheduled for Service 17 (including 4 Mobility Bus)

7wx	KJD507P	**88**ku	OJD888R	**139**m	THX139S	**268**k	YYE268T	**395**ux	BYW395V
9k	KJD509P	**96**ku	OJD896R	**150**k	THX150S	**293**m	YYE293T	**397**w	BYW397V
13k	KJD513P	**97**k	OJD897R	**153**k	THX153S	**297**k	YYE297T	**403**m	BYW403V
24k	KJD524P	**98**ku	OJD898R	**177**ux	THX177S	**304**ku	AYR304T	**405**ku	BYW405V
27u	KJD527P	**99**k	OJD899R	**195**dku	THX195S	**320**m	AYR320T	**408**ku	BYW408V
29k	KJD529P	**105**m	OJD905R	**201**u	THX201S	**335**k	AYR335T	**411**ux	BYW411V
30k	KJD530P	**112**k	THX112S	**227**ux	THX227S	**337**k	AYR337T	**422**ku	BYW422V
35k	KJD535P	**116**ku	THX116S	**243**u	THX243S	**363**kt	BYW363V	**429**ku	BYW429V
61w	OJD861R	**121**m	THX121S	**245**wx	THX245S	**373**ku	BYW373V	**431**a	BYW431V
71u	OJD871R	**122**u	THX122S	**251**k	THX251S	**381**k	BYW381V	**434**k	BYW434V
79w	OJD879R	**123**k	THX123S	**259**ux	THX259S	**385**k	BYW385V	**435**	BYW435V
84k	OJD884R								

a Surrey County Council centenary livery d DAF engine k Westlink livery m Mobility Bus
t Trainer u Unlicensed w Withdrawn x Docklands Express livery

LS 438-506

Sub-frames Leyland National 2 NL106L11/2R
Engine Leyland 0680 11.1-litre rated at 117kW at 1850rpm
Bodywork Leyland National B28D+46 (except LS 444/51/8/70/2/84/95/7, 503/4 are B44F and in route 607 livery; LS 459/64/73/83/5/6/91 are B36D+27)
Built 1981
Dimensions 10600mm x 2502mm x 3307mm
Number Built 69
Number in Stock 67
Number Scheduled for Service 46 (including 39 Red Arrow)

438	GUW438W	**452**	GUW452W	**468**gu	GUW468W	**481**gu	GUW481W	**494**	GUW494W
439gu	GUW439W	**453**	GUW453W	**469**gu	GUW469W	**482**	GUW482W	**495**	GUW495W
440	GUW440W	**455**	GUW455W	**470**	GUW470W	**483**a	GUW483W	**496**	WLT696
441	GUW441W	**456**	GUW456W	**471**u	GUW471W	**484**	GUW484W	**497**	GUW497W
442gu	GUW442W	**457**	GUW457W	**472**	GUW472W	**485**	GUW485W	**498**	GUW498W
443	WLT843	**458**u	GUW458W	**473**	GUW473W	**486**gu	GUW486W	**499**	GUW499W
444u	GUW444W	**459**a	GUW459W	**474**gu	GUW474W	**487**	WLT487	**500**	GUW500W
445	GUW445W	**460**	GUW460W	**475**u	GUW475W	**488**	GUW488W	**501**gu	GUW501W
446	GUW446W	**461**	GUW461W	**476**gu	GUW476W	**489**u	GUW489W	**502**	GUW502W
447	GUW447W	**462**	GUW462W	**477**	GUW477W	**490**	GUW490W	**503**	503CLT
448	WLT648	**463**	GUW463W	**478**	GUW478W	**491**gu	GUW491W	**504**	GUW504W
449u	GUW449W	**464**	GUW464W	**479**	GUW479W	**492**	GUW492W	**505**	GUW505W
450	GUW450W	**465**	GUW465W	**480**	VLT180	**493**	GUW493W	**506**gu	GUW506W
451au	GUW451W	**467**	GUW467W						

Named vehicle: LS 438 *City of London* g Under conversion to Greenway specification u Unlicensed

LX

Chassis Leyland Lynx LX112L10ZR1R (LX 1/2), LX2R11C15Z4S (LX 3-8), LX112TL11ZR1R (LX 9-11)
Engine Cummins L10-B210H 10-litre rated at 157kW at 1850rpm (LX 1/2), Cummins 6CT8.3 8.27-litre developing 211bhp at 2400rpm (LX 3-8), Leyland TL11H 11.1-litre rated at 157kW at 1850rpm (LX 9-11)
Bodywork Leyland B47F+22 (LX 1/2), B49F+22 (LX 3-8, 11), B51F+22 (LX 9-10)
Built 1987-1989
Dimensions 11180mm x 2502mm x 3129mm
Number Built 11 (including acquisitions)
Number in Stock 11
Number Scheduled for Service 10

1a	F101GRM	**4**	G74UYV	**6**	G76UYV	**8**	G78UYV	**10**a	810DYE
2a	F102GRM	**5**	G75UYV	**7**	G77UYV	**9**a	809DYE	**11**a	811DYE
3	G73UYV								

Previous owner: LX 9-11 Merthyr Tydfil in 1989   a Route 607 livery

MA

Chassis Mercedes-Benz 811D
Engine Mercedes-Benz OM364A 3.64-litre turbocharged rated at 85kW at 2600rpm
Bodywork Alexander 'AM' B28F+15 (except MA 2, 12, 34/6, 47, 51/5/6, 99, 100 are B26F+15, MA 101-5 are DP28F+15)
Built 1988-1991
Dimensions 8372mm x 2270mm x 2730mm
Number Built and in Stock 134
Number Scheduled for Service 103

1	F601XMS	**28**	F628XMS	**55**	F955BMS	**82**	F682XMS	**109**s	G109PGT
2	F602XMS	**29**	F629XMS	**56**	F656XMS	**83**	F683XMS	**110**s	G110PGT
3u	F603XMS	**30**	F630XMS	**57**	F657XMS	**84**	F684XMS	**111**s	G111PGT
4u	F604XMS	**31**	F631XMS	**58**	F658XMS	**85**	F685XMS	**112**s	G112PGT
5u	F605XMS	**32**	F632XMS	**59**	F659XMS	**86**	F686XMS	**113**s	G113PGT
6u	F606XMS	**33**	F633XMS	**60**	F660XMS	**87**	F687XMS	**114**s	G114PGT
7u	F607XMS	**34**	F634XMS	**61**	F661XMS	**88**	F688XMS	**115**s	G115PGT
8	F608XMS	**35**	F635XMS	**62**	F662XMS	**89**	F689XMS	**116**s	G116PGT
9	F609XMS	**36**	F636XMS	**63**	F663XMS	**90**	F690XMS	**117**s	G117PGT
10	F610XMS	**37**	F637XMS	**64**	F664XMS	**91**	F691XMS	**118**s	G118PGT
11	F611XMS	**38**	F638XMS	**65**	F665XMS	**92**	F692XMS	**119**s	G119PGT
12u	F612XMS	**39**	F639XMS	**66**	F666XMS	**93**	F693XMS	**120**s	G120PGT
13t	F613XMS	**40**	F640XMS	**67**	F667XMS	**94**	F694XMS	**121**s	G121PGT
14	F614XMS	**41**	F641XMS	**68**	F668XMS	**95**	F695XMS	**122**s	G122PGT
15	F615XMS	**42**	F642XMS	**69**	F669XMS	**96**	F696XMS	**123**s	G123PGT
16	F616XMS	**43**	F643XMS	**70**	F670XMS	**97**	F697XMS	**124**s	G124PGT
17	F617XMS	**44**	F644XMS	**71**	F671XMS	**98**	F698XMS	**125**s	H425XGK
18	F618XMS	**45**	F645XMS	**72**	F672XMS	**99**	F699XMS	**126**s	H426XGK
19	F619XMS	**46**	F946BMS	**73**	F673XMS	**100**	F700XMS	**127**s	H427XGK
20	F620XMS	**47**	F947BMS	**74**	F674XMS	**101**	VLT31	**128**s	H428XGK
21	F621XMS	**48**	F948BMS	**75**	F675XMS	**102**tu	F702XMS	**129**s	H429XGK
22	F622XMS	**49**	F949BMS	**76**	F676XMS	**103**	F703XMS	**130**s	H430XGK
23	F623XMS	**50**	F950BMS	**77**	F677XMS	**104**	F704XMS	**131**s	H431XGK
24	F624XMS	**51**	F951BMS	**78**	F678XMS	**105**	F705XMS	**132**s	H432XGK
25	F625XMS	**52**	F952BMS	**79**	F679XMS	**106**	F706XMS	**133**s	H433XGK
26	F626XMS	**53**	F953BMS	**80**	F680XMS	**107**	F707XMS	**134**s	H434XGK
27	F627XMS	**54**	F954BMS	**81**	F681XMS	**108**s	G108PGT		

s Streetline livery   t Trainer   u Unlicensed

MC

Chassis Mercedes-Benz 811D
Engine Mercedes-Benz OM364A 3.64-litre turbocharged rated at 85kW at 2600rpm
Bodywork Carlyle B28F+15
Built 1989-1990
Dimensions
Number Built and in Stock 5 (including acquisition)
Number Scheduled for Service 5

1	WLT491	**2**	H882LOX	**3**	H883LOX	**4**	WLT400	**5**	H885LOX

Previous owner: MC 1 Carlyle, Birmingham (demonstrator) in 1990

MR/MRL MR 1-63, MRL 65-92, MR 93-105, MRL 106-133, MR 134, MRL 135-241

Chassis MCW Metrorider MF150/14 (MR 1-17), MF150/18 (MR 20-22), MF150/38 (MR 23-52), MF150/46 (MR 53-63), MF158/1 (MRL 65-73), MF158/2 (MRL 74-76), MF158/18 (MRL 77), MF158/11 (MRL 78-88), MF158/12 (MRL 89-92), MF150/96 (MR 93-98), MF150/115 (MR 99-103), MF150/116 (MR 104/5), MF158/16 (MRL 106-131), MF158/17 (MRL 132/3), MF150/2 (MR 134), Optare Metrorider (MRL 135-241)
Engine Cummins 6B5.9 5.88-litre rated at 86kW at 2500rpm (MR/MRL 1-134), Cummins 6BT5.9 5.88-litre rated at 119kW at 2500rpm (MRL 135-241)
Bodywork Metro-Cammell-Weyman B23F+7 (MR 1-17, 99-103), DP25F+6 (MR 20-22), DP23F+7 (MR 104/5), B25F+6 (MR 23-63, 93-98, 134), B30F+16 (MR 65-73), DP33F+8 (MRL 74-76), B28F+14 (MRL 77-88, 106-131), DP31F+7 (MRL 89-92, 132/3), Optare B26F+14 (MRL 135-241)
Number Built 1987-1993
Dimensions 7040mm x 2210mm x 2750mm (MR), 8400mm x 2376mm x 2750mm (MRL)
Number in Stock 227 (64 MR, 163 MRL)
Number Scheduled for Service 157 (28 MR, 129 MRL)

1k	D461PON	59u	E635KYW	107	F107YVP	153	H153UUA	199	J699CGK
2k	D462PON	60u	E636KYW	108	F108YVP	154	H154UUA	200s	J710CGK
3k	D463PON	61u	E637KYW	109	F109YVP	155	H155UUA	201s	J701CGK
4k	D464PON	62w	E638KYW	110	F110YVP	156	H156UUA	202s	J702CGK
5k	D465PON	63u	E639KYW	111	F111YVP	157	H157UUA	203s	J703CGK
6k	D466PON	65	E641KYW	112	F112YVP	158	H158UUA	204s	J704CGK
7k	D467PON	66	E642KYW	113	F113YVP	159	H159UUA	205s	J705CGK
8u	D468PON	67	E643KYW	114	F114YVP	160	H160WWT	206s	J706CGK
9u	D469PON	68	E644KYW	115	F115YVP	161	H161WWT	207s	J707CGK
10k	D470PON	69	E645KYW	116	F116YVP	162	H162WWT	208s	J708CGK
11	D471PON	70u	E646KYW	117	F117YVP	163	H163WWT	209s	J709CGK
14w	D474PON	71u	E647KYW	118	F118YVP	164	H564WWR	210	J210BWU
16	D476PON	72	E648KYW	119	F119YVP	165	H165WWT	211	J211BWU
17	D477PON	73	E649KYW	120	F120YVP	166	H166WWT	212	J212BWU
20	D480PON	74u	E650KYW	121	F121YVP	167	H167WWT	213	J213BWU
21	D481PON	75u	E705LYU	122	F122YVP	168	H168WWT	214	J214BWU
22u	D482PON	76u	E706LYU	123	F123YVP	169	H169WWT	215	J215BWU
23k	E123KYW	77	F197YDA	124	F124YVP	170	H170WWT	216	J216BWU
25	E125KYW	78k	F182YDA	125	F125YVP	171	H171WWT	217	J217BWU
26	E126KYW	79k	F183YDA	126	F126YVP	172	H172WWT	218	J218BWU
27	E127KYW	80k	F184YDA	127	F127YVP	173	H173WWT	219	J219BWU
29	E129KYW	81k	F185YDA	128	F128YVP	174	H174WWT	220	J220BWU
30k	E130KYW	82k	F186YDA	129	F129YVP	175	H175WWT	221	J221BWU
31k	E131KYW	83k	F187YDA	130	F130YVP	176	H176WWT	222	K422HWY
33u	E133KYW	84k	F188YDA	131	F131YVP	177	VLT277	223s	K223MGT
34k	E134KYW	85k	F189YDA	132	F132YVP	178	H678YGO	224	K424HWY
35	E135KYW	86k	F190YDA	133	F133YVP	179	H679YGO	225	K425HWY
36	E136KYW	87k	F191YDA	134p	D482NOX	180	H680YGO	226	K426HWY
38w	E138KYW	88k	F192YDA	135	H135TGO	181	H681YGO	227	K427HWY
39k	E139KYW	89k	F193YDA	136	H136UUA	182	H682YGO	228	K428HWY
40	E140KYW	90k	F194YDA	137	H137UUA	183	H683YGO	229	K429HWY
41	E141KYW	91k	F195YDA	138	H138UUA	184	H684YGO	230	K430HWY
42k	E142KYW	92k	F196YDA	139	H139UUA	185	H685YGO	231	K431HWY
44	E144KYW	93	E873NJD	140	H140UUA	186	H686YGO	232	K432HWY
45	E145KYW	94	E874NJD	141	H141UUA	187	H687YGO	233	K433HWY
46	E146KYW	95	F895OYR	142	H142UUA	188	H688YGO	234	K434HWY
47	E147KYW	96	F896OYR	143	H143UUA	189	H689YGO	235	K435HWY
48	E148KYW	97	F897OYR	144	H144UUA	190	H690YGO	236	K436HWY
49	E149KYW	98	F898OYR	145	H145UUA	191	J691CGK	237	K437HWY
50	E150KYW	99	F99YVP	146	H146UUA	192	J692CGK	238	K438HWY
51	E151KYW	100	F100YVP	147	H147UUA	193	J693CGK	239	K439HWY
52k	E152KYW	102	F102YVP	148	H148UUA	194	J694CGK	240	K440HWY
53u	E929KYR	103	F103YVP	149	H149UUA	195	J695CGK	241	K441HWY
56w	E632KYW	104d	F104YVP	150	H150UUA	196	J696CGK		
57	E633KYW	105d	F105YVP	151	H151UUA	197	J697CGK		
58w	E634KYW	106	F106YVP	152	H152UUA	198	698DYE		

d DHSS Shuttle livery   k Westlink livery   p Kingston University livery   s Streetline livery   u Unlicensed   w Withdrawn

Previous owner: MR 134 MCW, Birmingham (demonstrator) in 1989

MT

Chassis Mercedes-Benz 709D
Engine Mercedes-Benz OM364 3.64-litre rated at 66kW at 2800rpm
Bodywork Reeve Burgess B20FL+5
Built 1988-1989
Dimensions 8400mm x 2320mm x 2900mm
Number Built and in Stock 7
Number Scheduled for Service 6

1s	F391DHL	**3**s	F393DHL	**5**s	F395DHL	**7**m	G537GBD	**8**m	G538GBD
2s	F392DHL	**4**s	F394DHL						

m Mobility Bus livery s Southall Shuttle livery

MTL

Chassis Mercedes-Benz 811D
Engine Mercedes-Benz OM364A 3.64-litre rated at 85kW at 2600rpm
Bodywork Reeve Burgess 'Beaver' B29F+15 (MTL 1, 3-5), B26F+15 (MTL 2), DP33F+7 (MTL 6)
Built 1989-1991
Dimensions 8430mm x 2320mm x 2894mm
Number Built and in Stock 6
Number Scheduled for Service 3

1	G621XLO	**3**	H189RWF	**5**a	H192RWF
2	G222KWE	**4**	H191RWF	**6**	VLT77

a On extended hire from Mercedes-Benz, Tankersley

MW

Chassis Mercedes-Benz 811D
Engine Mercedes-Benz OM364A 3.64-litre rated at 85kW at 2600rpm
Bodywork Wright B26F+15
Built 1989-1993
Dimensions 8220mm x 2340mm x 2930mm
Number Built and in Stock 37
Number Scheduled for Service 31

1	HDZ2601	**9**	HDZ2609	**17**a	LDZ9017	**24**	NDZ7924	**31**	NDZ7931
2	HDZ2602	**10**	HDZ2610	**18**	NDZ7918	**25**	NDZ7925	**32**	NDZ7932
3	HDZ2603	**11**	HDZ2611	**19**	NDZ7919	**26**	NDZ7926	**33**	NDZ7933
4	HDZ2604	**12**	HDZ2612	**20**	NDZ7920	**27**	NDZ7927	**34**	NDZ7934
5	HDZ2605	**13**	HDZ2613	**21**	NDZ7921	**28**	NDZ7928	**35**	NDZ7935
6	HDZ2606	**14**	HDZ2614	**22**	NDZ7922	**29**	NDZ7929	**36**	NDZ7936
7	HDZ2607	**15**	HDZ2615	**23**	NDZ7923	**30**	NDZ7930	**37**	NDZ7937
8	HDZ2608	**16**	HDZ2616						

a On extended hire from Wright, Belfast (demonstrator)

RB

Chassis Renault 75
Engine Perkins Phaser 110T 3.99-litre turbocharged rated at 80kW at 2600rpm
Bodywork Reeve Burgess 'Beaver' B29F+11 (RB1, 22-5 are DP29F+11)
Built 1989-1990
Dimensions 8261mm x 2300mm x 2850mm
Number Built and in Stock 33
Number Scheduled for Service 28

1	G871WML	**8**	G878WML	**15**	G885WML	**22**	G892WML	**29**	H129AML
2	G872WML	**9**	G879WML	**16**	G886WML	**23**	G893WML	**30**	H130AML
3	G873WML	**10**	G880WML	**17**	G887WML	**24**	G894WML	**31**	H131AML
4	G874WML	**11**	G881WML	**18**	G888WML	**25**	G895WML	**32**	H132AML
5	G875WML	**12**	G882WML	**19**	G889WML	**26**	H126AML	**33**	H133AML
6	G876WML	**13**	G883WML	**20**	G890WML	**27**	H127AML		
7	G877WML	**14**	G884WML	**21**	G891WML	**28**	H128AML		

RH

Chassis Fiat Iveco Daily 49-10
Engine Iveco 8140.27 2.45-litre turbocharged rated at 76kW at 3800rpm
Bodywork Robin Hood B21F+7 (RH 1 is DP21F+7)
Built 1986
Dimensions 6300mm x 2100mm x 2850mm
Number Built 24
Number in Stock 4

1r	C501DYM	**5**	C505DYM	**7**	C507DYM	**22**	D522FYL

r Roundabout livery

Named vehicles: RH 1 *Kestrel*, RH 5 *Owl*, RH 7 *Swallow*, RH22 *Hawk*

RW

Chassis Renault 50
Engine Perkins Phaser 110T 3.99-litre turbocharged rated at 80kW at 2600rpm
Bodywork Wright B28F+15 (RW 86-90 are DP28F+15)
Built 1990
Dimensions 8275mm x 2300mm x 2850mm
Number Built and in Stock 90
Number Scheduled for Service 78

1	HDZ5401	**19**	HDZ5419	**37**	HDZ5437	**55**	HDZ5455	**73**	HDZ5473
2	HDZ5402	**20**	HDZ5420	**38**	HDZ5438	**56**	HDZ5456	**74**	HDZ5474
3	HDZ5403	**21**	HDZ5421	**39**	HDZ5439	**57**	HDZ5457	**75**	HDZ5475
4	HDZ5404	**22**	HDZ5422	**40**	HDZ5440	**58**	HDZ5458	**76**	HDZ5476
5	HDZ5405	**23**	HDZ5423	**41**	HDZ5441	**59**	HDZ5459	**77**	HDZ5477
6	HDZ5406	**24**	HDZ5424	**42**	HDZ5442	**60**	HDZ5460	**78**	HDZ5478
7	HDZ5407	**25**	HDZ5425	**43**	HDZ5443	**61**	HDZ5461	**79**	HDZ5479
8	HDZ5408	**26**	HDZ5426	**44**	HDZ5444	**62**	HDZ5462	**80**	HDZ5480
9	HDZ5409	**27**	HDZ5427	**45**	HDZ5445	**63**	HDZ5463	**81**	HDZ5481
10	HDZ5410	**28**	HDZ5428	**46**	HDZ5446	**64**	HDZ5464	**82**	HDZ5482
11	HDZ5411	**29**	HDZ5429	**47**	HDZ5447	**65**	HDZ5465	**83**	HDZ5483
12	HDZ5412	**30**	HDZ5430	**48**	HDZ5448	**66**	HDZ5466	**84**	HDZ5484
13	HDZ5413	**31**	HDZ5431	**49**	HDZ5449	**67**	HDZ5467	**85**	HDZ5485
14	HDZ5414	**32**	HDZ5432	**50**	HDZ5450	**68**	HDZ5468	**86**	HDZ5486
15	HDZ5415	**33**	HDZ5433	**51**	HDZ5451	**69**	HDZ5469	**87**	HDZ5487
16	HDZ5416	**34**	HDZ5434	**52**	HDZ5452	**70**	HDZ5470	**88**	HDZ5488
17	HDZ5417	**35**	HDZ5435	**53**	HDZ5453	**71**	HDZ5471	**89**	HDZ5489
18	HDZ5418	**36**	HDZ5436	**54**	HDZ5454	**72**	HDZ5472	**90**	HDZ5490

SC

Chassis Freight Rover Sherpa 374
Engine Leyland 2.5-litre rated at 52kW at 4000rpm
Bodywork Carlyle B6F
Built 1987
Dimensions 5131mm x 2146mm x 2731mm
Number Built 2
Number in Stock 1

1	D585OOV	Training bus in blue livery

SLW

Chassis Scania N113CRL
Engine Scania DS11-74 11-litre turbocharged rated at 187kW at 2000rpm
Bodywork Wright 'Pathfinder 320' B38D
Built 1993
Number on Order 30

1	**7**	**13**	**19**	**25**
2	**8**	**14**	**20**	**26**
3	**9**	**15**	**21**	**27**
4	**10**	**16**	**22**	**28**
5	**11**	**17**	**23**	**29**
6	**12**	**18**	**24**	**30**

SR

Chassis Mercedes-Benz 811D
Engine Mercedes-Benz OM364A 3.64-litre turbocharged rated at 85kW at 2600rpm
Bodywork Optare B26F+15
Built 1988-1989
Dimensions 8430mm x 2242mm x 2894mm
Number Built 123
Number in Stock 122
Number Scheduled for Service 93

1	WLT461	**27**	F927YWY	**52**	F52CWY	**77**	F177FWY	**102**	G102KUB
2	E712LYU	**28**	F928YWY	**53**	F53CWY	**78**	F178FWY	**103**	G103KUB
3	E713LYU	**29**	F29CWY	**54**	F154FWY	**79**	F179FWY	**104**	G104KUB
4	E714LYU	**30**	F30CWY	**55**	F155FWY	**80**	F180FWY	**105**	G105KUB
5	F905YWY	**31**	F31CWY	**56**	F156FWY	**81**	F181FWY	**106**	G106KUB
6	F906YWY	**32**	F32CWY	**57**	F157FWY	**82**	G82KUB	**107**	G107KUB
7	F907YWY	**33**	F33CWY	**58**	F158FWY	**83**	G83KUB	**108**	G108KUB
8	F908YWY	**34**	F34CWY	**59**	F159FWY	**84**	G84KUB	**109**	G109KUB
9	F909YWY	**35**	F35CWY	**60**	F160FWY	**85**	G85KUB	**110**	G110KUB
11	F911YWY	**36**	F36CWY	**61**	F161FWY	**86**	G86KUB	**111**	G111KUB
12	F912YWY	**37**	F37CWY	**62**	F162FWY	**87**	G87KUB	**112**	G112KUB
13	F913YWY	**38**	F38CWY	**63**	F163FWY	**88**	G88KUB	**113**	G113KUB
14	F914YWY	**39**	F39CWY	**64**	F164FWY	**89**	G89KUB	**114**	G114KUB
15	F915YWY	**40**	F40CWY	**65**	F165FWY	**90**	G90KUB	**115**	G115KUB
16	F916YWY	**41**	F41CWY	**66**	F166FWY	**91**	G91KUB	**116**	G116KUB
17	F917YWY	**42**	F42CWY	**67**	F167FWY	**92**	G92KUB	**117**	G117KUB
18	F918YWY	**43**	F43CWY	**68**	F168FWY	**93**	G93KUB	**118**	G118KUB
19	F919YWY	**44**	F44CWY	**69**	F169FWY	**94**	G94KUB	**119**	G119KUB
20	F920YWY	**45**	F45CWY	**70**	F170FWY	**95**	G95KUB	**120**	G120KUB
21	F921YWY	**46**	F46CWY	**71**	F171FWY	**96**	G96KUB	**121**	G121KUB
22	F922YWY	**47**	F47CWY	**72**	F172FWY	**97**	G97KUB	**122**	G122SMV
23	F923YWY	**48**	F48CWY	**73**	F173FWY	**98**	G98KUB	**123**	G123SMV
24	F924YWY	**49**	F49CWY	**74**	F174FWY	**99**	G99KUB		
25	F925YWY	**50**	F50CWY	**75**	F175FWY	**100**	G100KUB		
26	F926YWY	**51**	F51CWY	**76**	F176FWY	**101**	G101KUB		

VN

Chassis Volvo B10B-58
Engine Volvo THD103KF 9.6-litre rated at 180kW at 2000rpm
Bodywork Northern Counties B40D+23
Built 1993
Dimensions 11802mm x 2502mm x 3100mm
Number in Stock 13
Number Scheduled for Service 11

1	K100KLL	**4**	K4KLL	**7**	K70KLL	**10**	K10KLL	**12**	K12KLL
2	K2KLL	**5**	K5KLL	**8**	K8KLL	**11**	K11KLL	**13**	K13KLL
3	K3KLL	**6**	K6KLL	**9**	K9KLL				

All are in Clapham Omnibus livery

COACHES

DD35	J35GCX	DAF SB2305DHS585	Duple 321	C57F	1992	
DD36	J36GCX	DAF SB2305DHS585	Duple 321	C57F	1992	
DP1	F637OHD	DAF MB230LB615	Plaxton Paramount 3500 3	C53F	1988	Ex C&H, Fleetwood, 1992
DV36	K536RJX	DAF MB230LT615	Van Hool Alizée	C51F	1993	
DV37	K537RJX	DAF MB230LT615	Van Hool Alizée	C51F	1993	
DV38	K538RJX	DAF MB230LT615	Van Hool Alizée	C51F	1993	
DV39	K539RJX	DAF MB230LT615	Van Hool Alizée	C51F	1993	
DV67	E648KCX	DAF MB230LB615	Van Hool Alizée	C53FT	1988	Ex Shaw, Silverdale, 1992
LD5	WGV867X	Leyland Leopard PSU5D/4R	Duple Dominant	C50F	1982	Ex Beeston, Hadleigh, 1992
LP5	JVF815V	Leyland Leopard PSU3E/4R	Plaxton Supreme	C49F	1979	Ex Cambus, 1989
LP6	JVF816V	Leyland Leopard PSU3E/4R	Plaxton Supreme	C49F	1979	Ex Cambus, 1989
SKY1	E469YWJ	Auwaerter N122/3	Neoplan Skyliner	CH57/20C	1988	Ex ILG, Ratby, 1991
TDL1	F789GNA	Leyland Tiger TRCTL11/3ARZ	Duple	C53F	1990	Ex Shearings, Wigan, 1993
TDL2	F791GNA	Leyland Tiger TRCTL11/3ARZ	Duple	C53F	1990	Ex Shearings, Wigan, 1993
TPL1	G661WMD	Leyland Tiger TRCTL11/3RZAM	Plaxton Paramount 3200 3	C53F	1989	
TPL2	G662WMD	Leyland Tiger TRCTL11/3RZAM	Plaxton Paramount 3200 3	C53F	1989	
TPL3	G100VMM	Leyland Tiger TRCTL10/3ARZA	Plaxton Paramount 3200 3	C57F	1990	
TPL5	G601XMD	Leyland Tiger TRCTL10/3ARZA	Plaxton Paramount 3200 3	C53F	1990	
TPL7	H642GRO	Leyland Tiger TRCL10/3ARZA	Plaxton Paramount 3200 3	C53F	1991	
TPL8	H643GRO	Leyland Tiger TRCL10/3ARZA	Plaxton Paramount 3200 3	C53F	1991	
VP1	G91RGG	Volvo B10M-60	Plaxton Paramount 3200 3	C53F	1990	Ex Park, Hamilton, 1993
VT1	YTA612S	Volvo B58-61	Duple Dominant	C53F	1977	Ex Brown, Horley, 1991

Ownership:
Selkent: DD35/6, DP1 , DV36-39, 67
Metroline: LD5, TDL1/2
Leaside: LP5/6, TPL1,2,8
East London: TPL3,5,7
London Northern: VP1, SKY1
Westlink: VT1

PREVIOUS REGISTRATIONS OF RE-REGISTERED VEHICLES

CV5	G195CHN	**L262**	D262FYL	**MRL177**	H677YGO	**RM1125**	125CLT
CV6	G196CHN	**L263**	D263FYL	**MRL198**	J698CGK	**RM1197**	197CLT
CV7	G197CHN	**LS443**	GUW443W	**MTL6**	F396DHL	**RM1217**	217CLT
DA1	WLT400	**LS448**	GUW448W	**RM9**	VLT9	**RM1292**	292CLT
DA2	F551SHX	**LS480**	GUW480W	**RM13**	VLT13	**RM1330**	330CLT
DR32	H532XGK	**LS487**	GUW487W	**RM14**	VLT14	**RM1352**	352CLT
DR46	H546XGK	**LS496**	GUW496W	**RM29**	VLT29	**RM1435**	435CLT
DT28	G28TGW	**LS503**	GUW503W	**RM46**	VLT46	**RM1545**	545CLT
DT32	G32TGW	**LX9**	D105NDW	**RM53**	VLT53	**RM1619**	619DYE
DT55	G55TGW	**LX10**	D106NDW	**RM98**	VLT98	**RM1621**	621DYE
DT168	H349GCK	**LX11**	D111NDW	**RM180**	VLT180	**RM1656**	656DYE
DW45	JDZ2345	**M188**	BYX188V	**RM244**	VLT244	**RM1698**	698DYE
DW46	JDZ2346	**M197**	BYX197V	**RM311**	WLT311	**RM1700**	700DYE
DW48	JDZ2348	**M198**	BYX198V	**RM346**	WLT346	**RM1809**	809DYE
DW52	JDZ2352	**M278**	BYX278V	**RM379**	WLT379	**RM1811**	811DYE
DW66	H366XGC	**M284**	BYX284V	**RM432**	WLT432	**RM1815**	815DYE
GLS2	FCA9X	**M379**	GYE379W	**RM463**	WLT463	**RM1836**	836DYE
L7	C807BYY	**M463**	GYE463W	**RM474**	WLT474	**RMC1486**	486CLT
L13	C813BYY	**M479**	GYE479W	**RM487**	WLT487	**SP18**	K318FYG
L16	C816BYY	**M542**	GYE542W	**RM548**	WLT548	**SR1**	E711LYU
L27	C27CHM	**M845**	545CLT	**RM554**	WLT554	**T1000**	A600THV
L33	C33CHM		OJD845Y	**RM648**	WLT648	**T1128**	WDA3T
L47	C47CHM	**M853**	OJD853Y	**RM696**	WLT696	**VC1**	G101NGN
L95	C95CHM	**M954**	A954SUL	**RM803**	WLT803	**VC3**	G103NGN
L151	D151FYM	**M1046**	A746THV	**RM837**	WLT837	**VC4**	G104NGN
L154	D154FYM	**M1315**	C315BUV	**RM843**	WLT843	**VC6**	G106NGN
L156	D156FYM	**M1379**	C379BUV	**RM916**	WLT916	**VC11**	G111NGN
L170	D170FYM	**M1389**	C389BUV	**RM1002**	2CLT	**VC14**	G114NGN
L172	D172FYM	**M1432**	C432BUV	**RM1005**	5CLT	**VC18**	G118NGN
L173	D173FYM	**M1434**	C434BUV	**RM1018**	18CLT	**VC19**	G119NGN
L180	D180FYM	**M1435**	C435BUV	**RM1019**	19CLT	**VC21**	G121NGN
L190	D190FYM	**M1436**	C436BUV	**RM1020**	20CLT	**VC23**	G123NGN
L215	D215FYM	**M1437**	C437BUV	**RM1023**	23CLT	**VC25**	G125NGN
L217	D217FYM	**MA101**	F903CMS	**RM1046**	46CLT	**VC29**	G129PGK
L219	D219FYM		F701XMS	**RM1078**	78CLT	**VC36**	G136PGK
L244	D244FYM	**MC1**	F430BOP	**RM1089**	89CLT	**VC37**	G137PGK
L260	D260FYL	**MC4**	H884LOX	**RM1101**	101CLT	**VC39**	J139DGF
L261	D261FYL						

SERVICE VEHICLES

The serial number is followed by a letter to indicate the builder or use of the vehicles. Suffixes currently in use are: B *(Bedford or Vauxhall)*, D *((Dodge)*, F *(Ford)*, L *(Leyland group)*, LR *(Land Rover)*, M *(Mercedes-Benz)*, P *(Peugeot)*, T *(Toyota)*, VW *(Volkswagen)*. Vehicles formerly marketed under the Bedford trading name are now generally sold as Vauxhalls; for a while, some of these were assigned V suffix codes, though no extant examples are now known.

1282F	580EYU	Thames 3ton auxiliary breakdown tender (preserved)	1963
1761LR	MGX913L	Land Rover	1972
1946F	KJD946P	D1010 box van (uniform issue unit)	1976
1947F	KJD947P	D1010 box van (uniform issue unit)	1976
1992F	OJD992R	D1010 box van (uniform issue unit)	1976
1993F	OJD993R	D1010 box van (uniform issue unit)	1976
2216B	CUC216V	TL1630 2450-gal fuel tanker	1979
2319F	CGT319X	D1210 tipper dropside	1981
2372L	MYL372X	Freighter recovery vehicle	1982
2378F	NYR378Y	Cargo 1011 dropside tail lift lorry	1983
2380F	NYR380Y	Cargo 1613 dropside lorry	1983
2383D	NYR383Y	G12 dropside lorry	1983
2384D	NYR384Y	G1085 crew cab box van with tail lift	1983
2385D	NYR385Y	G12 dropside lorry	1983
2395L	A395SJD	Freighter 1613 dropside lorry with crane	1983
2396F	A396SJD	Cargo 1613 dropside lorry	1983
2397L	A397SJD	Freighter 1613 dropside lorry with crane	1983
2398F	A398SJD	Cargo 1613 dropside lorry with crane	1983
2399F	A399SJD	Cargo 1613 dropside lorry	1983
2402D	A402SJD	G1085 crew cab dropside lorry with tail lift	1984
2404F	A404SJD	Cargo 1011 Box van	1983
2406D	A406SJD	G1085 crew cab dropside bolster lorry with tail lift	1984
2407F	A407SJD	Cargo 1613 dropside lorry	1983
2409D	A409SJD	G1285 crew cab with crane dropside lorry and generator	1983
2415L	B731XJD	Freighter T45 recovery truck	1984
2416L	B732XJD	Freighter T45 recovery truck	1984
2420D	B420XYU	G16 Refuse Collection truck	1985
2422L	B561YYN	Sherpa 350 Van	1985
2424D	C424BYH	S75 Truck with crew cab and dropside	1985
2427M	C715VOY	307D dropside truck	1986
2428M	C716VOY	307D dropside truck	1986
2430M	C718VOY	307D dropside truck	1986
2431M	C717VOY	307D truck	1986
2432M	C713VOY	307D truck	1986
2434F	C93WBY	Cargo 0811 curtainsided truck	1986
2435L	D295ECR	Freighter T45 dropside lorry with crane	1986
2437F	D206YLK	Cargo 1011 dropside truck with tail lift	1986
2439F	C95WBY	Cargo 1011 box van with tail lift	1986
2441F	C94WBY	Cargo 1011 box van with tail lift	1986
2442F	D203YLK	Cargo 0811 box truck	1986
2444F	C491WLW	Cargo 1913 artic unit	1986
2447M	C712WLB	307D Curtainsided truck	1986
2448M	C713WLB	307D Curtainsided truck	1986
2450M	C715WLB	307D Curtainsided truck	1986
2452M	C717WLB	307D Curtainsided truck	1986
2454M	C719WLB	307D Curtainsided truck	1986
2457B	D66ALO	Bedford Midi Van	1987
2460L	D646YDP	Sherpa 300 minibus	1987
2461L	D647YDP	Sherpa 300 minibus	1987
2464L	E693GLT	Freighter 1313 crew cab and tail lift lorry	1988
2465F	E845HLM	Cargo 0811 dropside truck	1988
2466F	E842HLM	Cargo 0811 dropside truck	1988
2467F	E843HLM	Cargo 0811 dropside truck	1988
2468F	E844HLM	Cargo 0811 dropside truck	1988
2469M	E307GLO	814 dropside truck	1987
2470M	E308GLO	814 dropside truck	1987
2471M	D543CLC	1625 articulated unit	1987
2472M	G384VJB	1617 articulated unit	1989
2473F	G239YLD	Transit dropside with crane	1989
2474M	G227YLT	1726 artic unit	1990
2475M	G921ALM	408B demountable chassis cab	1990
2476M	G922ALM	408B demountable chassis cab	1990
2477M	G923ALM	408B demountable chassis cab	1990
2478M	G924ALM	408B demountable chassis cab	1990
2480M	G926ALM	408B demountable chassis cab	1990
2481F	G776BLF	Transit dropside	1990
2482M	H327FLH	2421 dustcart	1990
2483M	H329FLH	2421 dustcart	1990
2484M	G794BLM	609D van	1990
2485M	H215FLB	814 dropside truck	1990
2486M	H217FLB	814 dropside truck	1990
2487M	H218FLB	814 dropside truck	1990
2488M	H219FLB	814 communications truck	1991
2489M	H220FLB	814 dropside truck	1990
2490M	H221FLB	814 box truck with tail lift	1990
2491M	H223FLB	814 box truck demountable	1990
2492M	H224FLB	814 box truck demountable	1990
2493M	H225FLB	814 box truck demountable	1990
2494M	H226FLB	814 box truck demountable	1990
2495M	H437GAN	814 box truck demountable	1990
2496M	H438GAN	814 box truck demountable	1990
2497M	K671PLH	410 demountable truck	1992
2498F	H208FLM	Cargo dropside truck with tail lift and winch	1990
2499F	H219FLM	Cargo dropside truck with tail lift and winch	1990
2502F	K251PLA	Transit 15-seat minibus	1992
2503F	K252PLA	Transit 15-seat minibus	1992
2504M	K672PLH	Caged truck	1993
2505F	K156PLY	Transit 12-seat minibus	1993
2506F	K157PLY	Transit 15-seat minibus	1993
2507F	K158PLY	Transit van	1993
2508M	K490RLA	1114 11-tonne demountable truck	1993
2509M	K489RLA	1114 11-tonne demountable truck	1993
2510M	K461RLA	410D curtain-side truck	1993
2511M	K462RLA	410D curtain-side truck	1993
2512F	K206RLO	Transit 190 high-top van	1993
2513F	K201RLO	Transit 190 high-top van	1993
2514F	K202RLO	Transit 190 high-top van	1993
2515F	K205RLO	Transit 190 high-top van	1993
2516F	K203RLO	Transit 190 high-top van	1993
2517F	K208RLO	Transit 190 high-top van	1993
2518F	K207RLO	Transit 190 high-top van	1993
2519F	K204RLO	Transit 190 high-top van	1993
2520F	K209RLO	Transit 190 high-top van	1993
2521F	K210RLO	Transit 190 high-top van	1993
2522F	K221RLO	Super Cargo 17-tonne dropside truck	1993
2523F	K229RLO	Super Cargo 17-tonne dropside truck	1993
2524F	K245RLO	Super Cargo 17-tonne dropside truck	1993
2525M	K479RLA	1520 articulated unit	1993
2526M	K480RLA	1520 articulated unit	1993
2527M	K477RLA	1520 articulated unit	1993
2528M	K478RLA	1520 articulated unit	1993
DM 1159	KUC159P	OPAL project base	
DMS 1515	THM515M	Supercar advertising vehicle	
RCL 2221	CUV221C	Mobile cinema and exhibition vehicle	
RM 811	WLT811	Mobile cinema and exhibition vehicle	

Leased Service Vehicles

No.	Registration	Vehicle	Year
3609F	F356YFX	Transit van	1989
3650F	C706TSO	Escort van	1988
3695F	F617OFE	Transit pick-up	1989
3743B	F133OCN	Astra van	1989
3744F	F793YLJ	Escort van	1989
3758F	F786NFE	Transit van	1989
3759F	F851XPR	Transit van	1989
3774F	G956CLJ	Transit van	1989
3775F	G957CLJ	Transit van with crew cab	1989
3783F	F817YLJ	Transit van	1989
3786B	G517XRV	Astra van	1990
3792B	G506XRV	Astra van	1990
3797B	G518XRV	Astra van	1990
3803B	G505XRV	Astra estate	1990
3805B	G504XRV	Astra estate	1990
3812B	G631XBK	Astra estate	1990
3813B	G633XBK	Astra estate	1990
3822F	G317DFX	Escort van	1990
3829F	G845YNM	Transit van with crew cab	1990
3830F	G830ELJ	Transit van with crew cab	1990
3836F	G972FOA	Escort van	1989
3838F	G686DLJ	Escort van	1990
3840F	G914CLJ	Escort van	1990
3841F	G913CLJ	Escort van	1989
3842F	G843FEL	Transit van	1990
3843F	G598YNK	Transit van	1990
3844F	G597YNK	Transit van	1990
3848F	G565VNM	Transit van	1990
3849F	G849YNM	Transit van	1990
3850F	G852YNM	Transit van	1990
3851F	G568VNM	Transit minibus	1990
3852F	G391XVS	Transit van	1990
3853F	G571VNM	Transit van	1990
3855F	G299WNM	Transit van	1990
3856F	G301WNM	Transit van	1990
3857F	G396XVS	Transit van	1990
3858F	G388XVS	Transit van	1990
3859F	G563VNM	Transit dropside truck	1990
3862F	G256GNP	P100 pick-up	1990
3864F	G868ADG	Escort estate	1989
3865F	G867ADG	Escort estate	1989
3866F	G708DLJ	Transit van	1990
3870F	G277GNP	Fiesta van	1990
3873F	H904JEL	Transit van	1990
3875B	G568VYN	Astra estate	1990
3878P	G838UUD	504 pick-up truck	1990
3879F	E856EUT	Transit van	1990
3880F	D956OOB	Transit van	1990
3882B	H539OVF	Midi minibus	1990
3883B	H123YCU	Mini minibus	1990
3885F	G778HUK	Fiesta van	1990
3887F	G801BDF	Transit van	1990
3888F	G824JDA	Transit van	1990
3890F	G536TNX	Transit van	1990
3891F	G658JOB	P100 pick-up truck	1990
3892F	G657JOB	P100 pick-up truck	1990
3893F	G659JOB	P100 pick-up truck	1990
3895F	H817YEW	Escort van	1990
3896B	G355EHK	Astra estate	1990
3897B	G354EHK	Astra estate	1990
3898F	G472YUR	Escort estate	1990
3899F	H395FAD	Escort estate	1990
3900F	H404FAD	Escort estate	1990
3901F	H398FAD	Escort estate	1990
3902F	H396FAD	Escort estate	1990
3903F	G521JDA	Escort van	1990
3904F	H275CKX	Escort van	1990
3905F	H276CKX	Escort van	1990
3906F	H815YEW	Escort van	1990
3907F	G432UDH	Transit Luton van	1990
3908F	H872BHA	Transit minibus	1990
3909F	H650LOP	Escort van	1990
3910F	G353JWP	Escort van	1990
3911F	G896KNP	Escort van	1990
3912F	H649LOP	Escort van	1990
3913F	G355JWP	Escort van	1990
3914F	H920KOV	Escort van	1990
3915F	G273UWD	Transit van	1990
3916F	H338AUE	Transit van	1990
3917F	G274UWD	Transit van	1990
3918F	H401FAD	Escort estate	1990
3919F	H403FAD	Escort estate	1990
3920F	H402FAD	Escort estate	1990
3921F	G865DDG	Escort estate	1990
3922F	H625CNX	Transit van	1990
3923F	G431UDH	Transit van	1990
3924F	H619CNX	Transit van	1990
3925F	H618CNX	Transit van	1990
3928F	H870BHA	Transit van	1990
3929F	H347AUE	Transit van	1990
3930F	H339AUE	Transit van	1990
3931F	H364AUE	Transit van	1990
3932F	H709BUE	Transit van	1990
3933F	H710BUE	Transit van	1990
3934F	H711BUE	Transit van	1990
3935F	H875BHA	Transit van	1990
3936F	G895JDA	Transit van	1990
3937F	H876BHA	Transit van	1990
3938F	H791LDA	Transit van	1990
3939F	H874BHA	Transit van	1990
3940F	H873BHA	Transit van	1990
3941F	H869BHA	Transit van	1990
3942F	H937CBH	Escort saloon	1990
3943B	G846WVK	Astramax van	1990
3944B	G847WVK	Astramax van	1990
3945F	G249UWD	Transit minibus	1990
3946F	G269BLW	Transit van	1990
3947F	G270BLW	Transit van	1990
3949F	G272BLW	Transit van	1990
3950F	G640YLW	Transit van	1990
3952F	H866ELP	Transit van	1990
3953F	G273BLW	Transit van	1990
3954F	G274BLW	Transit van	1990
3955F	G268BLW	Transit van	1990
3956F	H864ELP	Transit van	1990
3957F	G282BLW	Transit van	1990
3959F	G284BLW	Transit van	1990
3960F	G285BLW	Transit van	1990
3961F	G286BLW	Transit van	1990
3962F	G629JOA	Fiesta van	1990
3963F	G362JWP	Fiesta van	1990
3964B	H569ATY	Astra estate	1990
3965B	G919XJR	Astra van	1991
3967F	H871BHA	Transit van	1990
3968F	G742JOB	Transit van	1990
3969F	H871ELP	Transit van	1990
3970F	G534TNX	Transit van	1990
3971T	G159UKE	Spacecruiser minibus	1990
3972F	G499GOJ	Transit van	1990
3973F	G498GOJ	Transit van	1990
3974F	H938JEL	Transit van	1990
3975F	H937JEL	Transit van	1990
3976F	H570KEL	Transit van	1991
3977F	G514JOA	Escort van	1990
3978F	G513JOA	Escort van	1990
3979F	H729JLJ	Transit dropside truck	1990
3980F	H731JLJ	Transit minibus	1990
3981F	F571TLO	Escort estate	1990
3982F	G618HWP	Escort van	1990
3983F	G617HWP	Escort van	1990
3984F	G892JDA	Escort van	1990
3985F	G220KAB	Escort estate	1990
3986B	G906YRV	Astra van	1990
3987B	G907YRV	Astra van	1990
3988B	G908YRV	Astra van	1990
3989F	H627CNX	Transit van	1990
3990F	G641ABH	Transit van	1990
3991F	G371JOK	Escort van	1990
3992F	G370JOK	Transit van	1990
3993F	G640ABH	Transit van	1990
3994F	G397XVS	Escort van	1990
3995F	G681UNX	Transit minibus	1990
3996F	H277CKX	Escort van	1990
3997F	H278CKX	Escort van	1990

3998F	H521DTM	Transit minibus	1990
3999B	H262BCR	Astra van	1990
4000F	F135SLK	Transit van	1990
4001F	H411MOK	Transit minibus	1990
4002F	G234RGX	Transit van	1990
4003F	H617CNX	Transit van	1990
4004B	H331CCR	Astra van	1990
4005F	H894MOK	Transit van	1991
4006F	H895MOK	Transit van	1991
4007F	H893MOK	Transit van	1991
4009F	H892MOK	Transit van	1991
4010B	H829DRV	Astra van	1991
4011B	H828DRV	Astra van	1991
4012B	H826DRV	Astra van	1991
4013F	H779FLL	Transit dropside truck	1990
4014F	H636GLE	Transit van	1991
4015F	H637GLE	Transit van	1991
4016F	H633GLE	Transit van	1991
4017F	H632GLE	Transit van	1991
4018F	H631GLE	Transit van	1991
4020F	H534GLE	Transit van	1991
4021F	H871LDA	Fiesta van	1991
4022B	H462WJX	Astra estate	1991
4023F	H357HNK	Escort van	1991
4024F	H945LDA	Escort estate	1991
4025B	H263BCR	Rascal van	1990
4026F	H628CNX	Transit van	1990
4027F	H477MOK	Transit van	1990
4028F	H679EKX	Transit dropside truck	1990
4029F	H403MOK	Escort van	1990
4030F	H476MOK	P100 pick-up truck	1990
4031B	F730HSU	Astra van	1990
4032F	H364DFK	Transit van	1990
4033B	H448DPX	Astra van	1991
4034B	H449DPX	Astra van	1991
4035B	H451DPX	Astra van	1991
4036B	H452DPX	Astra van	1991
4037B	H453DPX	Astra van	1991
4038B	H454DPX	Astra van	1991
4040F	H156GPV	Escort estate	1991
4041F	H155GPV	Escort estate	1991
4042F	H664VPW	Escort estate	1991
4044F	H187HRO	Escort van	1991
4045F	H189HRO	Escort van	1991
4046F	H182HRO	Escort van	1991
4047F	H183HRO	Escort van	1991
4048F	H184HRO	Escort van	1991
4049F	H185HRO	Escort van	1991
4050F	J722MRO	Escort van	1991
4051F	J723MRO	Escort van	1991
4052F	J724MRO	Escort van	1991
4053F	J725MRO	Escort van	1991
4054F	H949TUY	Escort van	1991
4055F	H947TUY	Escort van	1991
4056F	J822NMJ	Escort saloon	1991
4057F	H991ODA	Fiesta van	1991
4058F	H993ODA	Fiesta van	1991
4059F	H584SWP	Fiesta van	1991
4060F	H992ODA	Fiesta van	1991
4061F	H948TUY	Fiesta van	1991
4062F	H990ODA	Fiesta van	1991
4063F	H192HRO	Escort van	1991
4064F	H811JUR	Escort van	1991
4065F	H586SWP	Escort estate	1991
4066F	J726MRO	Escort van	1991
4067F	H813JUR	Escort van	1991
4068F	J382AAB	Escort estate	1991
4069F	J349AAB	Fiesta saloon	1991
4070F	H814JUR	Escort van	1991
4071F	H815JUR	Escort van	1991
4072F	J739MRO	Transit van	1991
4073F	J253KLW	Transit van	1991
4074B	H638EOT	Astra van	1991
4075B	H646EOT	Astra van	1991
4076B	H639EOT	Astra van	1991
4077B	H272KJX	Astra estate	1991
4078B	H645EOT	Astra L van	1991
4079B	H851GBA	Astra estate	1991
4080B	J939OPJ	Astra estate	1991
4081P	J661KOY	504 van	1991
4083P	H566HLU	504 van	1991
4084F	H460HLT	Escort estate	1991
4085F	H356HNK	Fiesta van	1991
4086F	H181HRO	Escort van	1991
4088F	J744MRO	Transit van	1991
4091F	H816JUR	Escort van	1991
4092F	J729MRO	Escort van	1991
4094F	H817JUR	Escort van	1991
4095VW	J768NGS	Transporter van	1991
4096F	J252KLW	Transit van	1991
4097F	J730MRO	Transit dropside	1991
4098F	H523OOP	Escort van	1991
4099F	J305KLW	Transit van	1991
4100F	J740MRO	Transit minibus	1991
4101F	J731MRO	Fiesta van	1991
4102F	J732MRO	Fiesta van	1991
4103F	J994ROC	Fiesta van	1991
4104B	J349GOW	Midi van	1991
4105B	J350GOW	Midi van	1991
4106F	J727MRO	Escort van	1991
4107F	J571ROK	Fiesta van	1991
4108F	J746MRO	Transit van	1991
4109F	J749MRO	Transit van	1992
4110F	J266LLT	Transit pick-up	1992
4111F	J267LLT	Transit pick-up	1992
4112F	J743MRO	P100 pick-up	1991
4113F	J717PKX	Transit van	1992
4114F	J716PKX	Transit van	1992
4115F	J715PKX	Transit van	1992
4116F	K252WNK	Transit van	1992
4117F	J836MLN	Transit van	1992
4118F	J834MLN	Transit van	1992
4119F	J835MLN	Transit van	1992
4120F	J719PKX	Transit van	1992
4121F	J810MLN	Transit van	1992
4122F	J754PKX	Transit van	1992
4123F	J706PKX	Transit van	1992
4124F	J705PKX	Transit van	1991
4125F	J718PKX	Transit van	1992
4126F	J710PKX	Transit van	1992
4127F	J260LLT	Transit van	1992
4128F	J262LLT	Transit van	1992
4130F	J850MLN	Transit minibus	1992
4131F	J713PKX	Transit van	1992
4132F	J712PKX	Transit van	1992
4133F	J263LLT	Transit minibus	1992
4134F	J711PKX	Transit minibus	1992
4135F	J704PKX	Escort van	1992
4136F	J78FGX	Escort van	1992
4137F	J532SVP	Escort van	1991
4138F	J128FMY	Escort van	1992
4139F	J769MRO	Escort van	1992
4142B	J898KFT	Astra van	1992
4143B	J255JRG	Astra estate	1991
4144B	J899KFT	Astra estate	1992
4145P	J265RPG	205 van	1992
4146F	J714PKX	Transit van	1992
4148F	J969MBY	Transit dropside	1992
4149F	J728MRO	P100 pick-up	1992
4150F	J748MRO	Fiesta van	1992
4151F	J764MRO	Escort van	1991
4152F	J761MRO	Escort van	1992
4153F	J762MRO	Escort van	1991
4154F	J763MRO	Escort van	1992
4155F	J709PKX	Transit van	1992
4156F	H815TWJ	Transit van	1992
4157F	H620RKU	Transit tipper	1992
4159F	J723PKX	Escort van	1992
4160F	J51TFL	Escort van	1992
4161F	J52TFL	Transit van	1992
4162F	J53TFL	Escort van	1992
4163F	J291VAV	Escort van	1992
4164F	J47TFL	Escort estate	1992
4165F	J46TFL	Escort estate	1992
4166F	J59TFL	Escort van	1992
4167F	J292VAV	Escort van	1992

4168VW	J362WCF	Transporter van	1992
4169VW	J363WCF	Transporter van	1992
4170F	K607OBY	Transit van	1992
4171F	J977MBY	Transit van	1992
4172F	K606OBY	Transit van	1992
4173F	K598OBY	Transit van	1992
4174F	K596OBY	Transit van	1992
4175F	K597OBY	Transit van	1992
4176F	K603OBY	Transit van	1992
4177F	K595OBY	Transit van	1992
4178F	J129NLD	Transit van	1992
4179F	J128NLD	Transit van	1992
4180F	J133NLD	Transit van	1992
4181F	J132NLD	Transit van	1992
4182F	K604OBY	Transit van	1992
4183F	J24TNM	Transit van	1992
4184F	J148NLD	Transit van	1992
4185F	K602OBY	Transit van	1992
4186F	K599OBY	Transit van	1992
4187F	J767OKX	Fiesta van	1992
4188F	J766PKX	Fiesta van	1992
4189F	K254WNK	Fiesta van	1992
4190F	J765PKX	Fiesta van	1992
4191F	J773PKX	Escort van	1992
4192F	J769PKX	Escort van	1992
4193F	J768PKX	Escort van	1992
4194F	J770PKX	Escort van	1992
4195F	J771PKX	Escort van	1992
4196F	K601PBY	Transit dropside	1992
4197F	J141NLD	Transit van	1992
4198F	K258WNK	Escort van	1992
4199F	J152NLD	Transit crewbus	1992
4200F	J151NLD	Transit crewbus	1992
4201F	K605OBY	Transit crewbus	1992
4202F	J825SMJ	Escort estate	1992
4203F	K255WNK	Fiesta van	1992
4204F	K257WNK	P100 pick-up	1992
4205F	K298OLW	Pick up with tail-lift	1993
4206P	K291OLW	Pick-up with tail-lift	1993
4207P	K292OLW	Pick-up	1993
4208P	K297OLW	Pick-up	1993
4209P	K364OLW	Pick-up	1993
4211B	K455MOT	Midi van	1993
4212B	J430MCN	Astra van	1992
4213B	J728LTY	Astra hatchback	1992
4214B	J725LTY	Astra van	1992
4215B	J726LTY	Astra van	1992
4216L	K182WUL	Leyland DAF Sherpa van	1992
4217F	K886XVS	Transit van	1993
4218F	K887XVS	Transit van	1993
4219F	K889XVS	Transit van	1993
4221F	J372TPP	Escort van	1992
4222F	J371TPP	Escort van	1992
4223F	J56TNM	Escort van	1992
4224F	J54TNM	Escort van	1992
4225F	J53TNM	Escort van	1992
4226T	J828VCK	Previa estate	1992
4227F	J52TNM	Escort van	1992
4228F	J51TNM	Escort van	1992
4229F	K907WNK	Escort van	1992
4230F	K908WNK	Escort van	1992
4231F	K909WNK	Escort van	1992
4232F	K910WNK	Escort van	1992
4233F	K601WVS	Escort estate	1992
4234F	K945WNK	Escort van	1992
4235B	K47VPF	Astramax van	1992
4236F	K259WNK	Fiesta van	1992
4238P	K165DKV	205 van	1993
4239F	K404XNK	Transit van	1993
4240F	K711XBW	Transit crewcab dropside truck	1993
4241F	K135YNM	Escort 5-door estate	1993
4242F	K718KWP	Escort 5-door hatchback	1993
4243F	K855XVS	Transit van	1993
4244F	K564VPC	Transit dropside	1993
4245F	K867XVS	Transit van	1993
4246P	K130AWK	Pick-up	1992
4247F	K713KWP	Escort estate	1992
4248F	K485WNM	Escort estate	1992
4250F	K781FWE	Transit van	1993
4251F	K782FWE	Transit van	1993
4252F	K783FWE	Transit van	1993
4256F	K785FWE	Transit van	1993
4257F	K786FWE	Transit van	1993
4258F	K787FWE	Transit van	1993
4259F	K788FWE	Transit van	1993
4260F	K789FWE	Transit dropside	1993
4264F	K902XVS	Escort van	1993
4265F	K901XVS	Escort van	1993
4266F	K941XVS	Escort van	1993
4267F	K942XVS	Escort van	1993
4275F	K798FWE	Escort van	1993
4276B	K828FWJ	Astra van	1993
4277B	K986PVK	Astra van	1993
4278B	K992PVK	Astra van	1993
4279B	K574NPO	Astra 5-door estate	1993
4280B	K573NPO	Astra 5-door estate	1993
4281F	K799FWE	Fiesta van	1993
4282F	K804FWE	Escort 5-door estate	1993
4285F	K635KUY	Escort van	1993
4286F	K631KGU	Escort van	1993
4287B	K926PVK	Astra van	1993
4288B	K942SDR	Midi van	1993
4289F	K922AJW	Transit crewcab dropside truck	1993
4290F	K925AJW	Transit crewcab dropside truck	1993
4293F	K932XVS	Transit van	1993
4294F	K931XVS	Transit van	1993
4295F	K389TAD	Escort van	1993
4296F	K926MNP	Escort van	1993
4297F	K864NAB	Escort estate car	1993
4299F	K408XNK	Escort van	1993

Vehicles held by LBL subsidiaries

	LHV340P	Austin taxicab	1976
	DLK263Y	Ford Transit van	1983
	TJH268Y	Land Rover	1983
	A966KEH	Ford Transit pick-up truck	1984
	B174CJX	Vauxhall Astra van	1984
	B738OLF	Ford Transit van	1985
	D732CAB	Ford Escort estate	1986
	D125PBW	Talbot Express	1986
	F518RYN	Ford Transit van	1988
PM1	F548RYN	Ford Transit van	1988
SM1	F413SLE	Mercedes-Benz 609D van	1989
	F810SLU	Leyland DAF Sherpa LWB van	1989
	F812SLU	Leyland DAF Sherpa LWB van	1989
	F524TLK	Ford Escort estate	1989
	G955TVS	Ford Transit van	1989
	G494WLH	Leyland DAF Sherpa LWB van	1989
	H741GLW	Ford Escort van	1991
	H742GLW	Ford Escort van	1991
	H743GLW	Ford Escort van	1991
	H744GLW	Ford Transit van	1991
	H812GNM	Vauxhall Astra van	1991
	H36GPP	Vauxhall Astra estate	1991
	J884KLR	Ford Fiesta van	1991
2	J522LLU	Ford Fiesta van	1991
LGF1	K781MGK	Ford Escort 1.8D van	1993
LGF2	K782MGK	Ford Transit 75 van	1993
LGF3	K783MGK	Ford Transit 75 van	1993
LGF4	K784MGK	Ford Transit 75 van	1993
LGF5	K785MGK	Ford Transit 75 van	1993
LGF6	K786MGK	Ford Transit 75 van	1993

GARAGES

The present system of allocating code letters to London bus garages was introduced late in 1911 when LGOC garages were given alphabetical codes from A to Y, excluding I, L and O. Many of the original garages have since been closed. New garages opened in 1913/4 were given two-letter codes starting with AB for Twickenham (closed 1970).

Three garages owned by LGOC were in use by Thomas Tilling up to 1933 and were prefixed by the letter T, these being TB (Bromley), TC (Croydon) and TL (Catford). LGOC type stencils were not carried until the opening of Bromley garage in 1924.

From 1924, new and acquired bus garages received codes related to their names. Trolleybus depots were allocated code letters in July 1950 and some names were then changed to avoid confusion with nearby bus garages; for example, Hackney was renamed Clapton and Holloway became Highgate. (The latter reverted to its original name after the closure of J garage in 1971.)

Through the years the facilities at garages have been updated continually, and from time to time major reconstructions have been carried out. However, as a result of service reductions in recent years, a large surplus of capacity has developed and several garages have been closed. The most recent examples are Edgware, Hanwell, Ash Grove, Seven Kings, Streatham and West Ham, with closure planned at Peckham and Victoria. Open-field sites have been created for midibus operation, most recently at Edgware, Greenford, Stratford and Wood Lane, with another to follow at Peckham.

LONDON CENTRAL BUSES
1 Warner Road, Camberwell, SE5 9LU

BX	BEXLEYHEATH	Erith Road, Bexleyheath	1935
NX	NEW CROSS	208 New Cross Road, SE14	1906
PM	PECKHAM	Peckham High Street, SE15	1951
Q	CAMBERWELL	Warner Road, SE5	1914

SOUTH EAST LONDON & KENT BUS COMPANY
Riverdale Offices, 68 Molesworth Street, Lewisham, SE13 7EU

OB	ORPINGTON	Unit A5, Nugent Industrial Estate, Cray Avenue, Orpington	1988
PD	PLUMSTEAD	Plumstead Road, SE28	1981
TB	BROMLEY	111 Hastings Road, Bromley	1924
TL	CATFORD	Bromley Road, Catford, SE26	1914

SOUTH LONDON TRANSPORT
Sycamore House, 799 London Road, Thornton Heath, CR4 6AW

BN	BRIXTON	39 Streatham Hill, SW2	1892
N	NORWOOD	Knights Hill, SE27	1909
TC	CROYDON	Brighton Road, Croydon	1916
TH	THORNTON HEATH	719 London Road, Thornton Heath	1879

LONDON GENERAL TRANSPORT SERVICES
London General House, 25 Raleigh Gardens, Mitcham, CR4 3NS

A	SUTTON	Bushey Road, Sutton	1924
AF	PUTNEY	Chelverton Road, SW15	1888
AL	MERTON	High Street, Colliers Wood, SW19	1913
GB	VICTORIA BASEMENT	Gillingham Street, SW1 (Central Minibus Unit)	1940
GM	VICTORIA	Gillingham Street, SW1	1940
RA	WATERLOO	Cornwall Road, SE1 (Red Arrow Unit)	1990
SW	STOCKWELL	Binfield Road, SW4	1952

LONDON UNITED BUSWAYS
Wellington Road, Twickenham, TW2 5NX

AV	HOUNSLOW	Kingsley Road, Hounslow	1913
B	WOOD LANE	Wood Lane, W12 (midibus site)	1992
FW	FULWELL	Stanley Road, Teddington	1902
S	SHEPHERDS BUSH	Wells Road, W12	1923
V	STAMFORD BROOK	72-74 Chiswick High Road, W4	1883

CENTREWEST
12th floor, Telstar House, Eastbourne Terrace, W2 6LG

AT	ACTON	Tram Depot, Uxbridge Road, Acton, W3	1990
G	GREENFORD	Greenford Road, Greenford (midibus site)	
ON	ALPERTON	Ealing Road, Alperton	1939
UX	UXBRIDGE	Bakers Road, Uxbridge	1983
X	WESTBOURNE PARK	Great Western Road, W9	1981

METROLINE TRAVEL
118-122 College Road, Harrow, HA1 1DB

AC	WILLESDEN	High Road, Willesden, NW10	1912
EW	EDGWARE	Station Road, Edgware (outstation)	1993
HD	HARROW WEALD	467 High Road, Harrow Weald	1930
NW	NORTH WEMBLEY	East Lane, North Wembley (midibus site)	1987
W	CRICKLEWOOD	Edgware Road, Dollis Hill, NW2	1905

LONDON NORTHERN BUS COMPANY
2nd floor, Hobson House, 155 Gower Street, WC1E 6LB

CF	CHALK FARM	Harmood Street, NW1	1916
FY	FINCHLEY	679 High Road, N12	1905
HT	HOLLOWAY	37A Pemberton Gardens, N19	1907
PB	POTTERS BAR	High Street, Potters Bar	1930

LEASIDE BUS COMPANY
Manor House Offices, 279 Seven Sisters Road, N4 1QG

AD	PALMERS GREEN	Regents Avenue, N13	1912
AR	TOTTENHAM	Philip Lane, High Cross, N15	1913
CT	CLAPTON	15 Bohemia Place, Mare Street, E8	1907
E	ENFIELD	Southbury Road, Ponders End	1928
SF	STAMFORD HILL	Rookwood Road, N16	1906
WN	WOOD GREEN	Jolly Butchers Hill, High Road, N22	1904

EAST LONDON BUS & COACH COMPANY
16-20 Clements Road, Ilford, IG1 1BA

BK	BARKING	205 Longbridge Road, Barking	1913
BW	BOW	Fairfield Road, E3	1908
NS	ROMFORD	North Street, Romford	1953
SD	STRATFORD	Waterden Road (midibus site)	1992
T	LEYTON	High Road, Leyton Green, E10	1912
U	UPTON PARK	Redclyffe Road, E6	1907

STANWELL BUSES (Westlink)
Unit 6, Pulborough Way, Green Lane, Hounslow TW4 6DE

K	KINGSTON	Cromwell Road, Kingston	1922
WK	WESTLINK	Unit 6, Pulborough Way, Green Lane, Hounslow	1986

VEHICLES SCHEDULED

A	SUTTON	DW (4), MRL (6), M (75)	85
AC	WILLESDEN	DR (2), DT (12), LN (11), M (34), RML (43)	102
AD	PALMERS GREEN	M (52)	52
AF	PUTNEY	M (23), MA (18), RML (33)	74
AL	MERTON	DR (14), DW (18), M (74), MRL (7)	113
AR	TOTTENHAM	M (45), RML (45)	90
AT	ACTON TOWN	M (20)	20
AV	HOUNSLOW	DR (24), DRL (13), DT (20), FR (7), M (47)	111
B	WOOD LANE	DR (29)	29
BK	BARKING	DA (24), DW (23), DWL (11), T (49)	107
BN	BRIXTON	M (35), RM (11), RML (23)	69
BW	BOW	RML (26), S (15), T (52)	93
BX	BEXLEYHEATH	MRL (24), MTL (3), T (58)	85
CF	CHALK FARM	DRL, (18), M (11), RM (16)	45
CT	CLAPTON	M (11), RML (37)	48
E	ENFIELD	M (83)	83
EW	EDGWARE	DR (11), M (7), SR (17)	35
FW	FULWELL	DR (28), DT (32), M (35)	95
FY	FINCHLEY	M (30), RML (21)	51
G	GREENFORD	MA (7), MT (4), RW (78)	89
GB	VICTORIA BASEMENT	DRL (18), MA (5), MRL (19), SR (21)	63
GM	VICTORIA	M (19), RM (22), RML (14)	55
HD	HARROW WEALD	M (37)	37
HT	HOLLOWAY	M (84), MRL (11), RM (1), RML (17), S (8)	121
K	KINGSTON	DWL (12), LS (2), MR (12), MRL (14), T (13)	53
N	NORWOOD	DR (10), L (34), M (7), MR (12), MRL (5), RML (16), SR (12)	96
NS	NORTH STREET	DW (10), LS (2), T (69)	81
NW	NORTH WEMBLEY	DT (41)	41
NX	NEW CROSS	L (14), SR (6), T (65)	85
OB	ORPINGTON	DT (12), FM (10), MC (5)	27
ON	ALPERTON	DW (13), MA (17), M (34)	64
PB	POTTERS BAR	M (44), MW (17), S (11)	72
PD	PLUMSTEAD	L (77), MA (11), MRL (11), T (20)	119
PM	PECKHAM	DRL (15), LS (2), MR (4), RM (27), RML (35), SR (9), T (29)	121
Q	CAMBERWELL	RM (9), RML (21), SP (24), SR (5), T (55)	114
RA	WATERLOO RED ARROW	GLS (1), LS (39)	40
S	SHEPHERDS BUSH	M (16), RML (37)	53
SD	STRATFORD	MRL (14), RB (28)	42
SF	STAMFORD HILL	L (35), M (31)	66
SW	STOCKWELL	DR (7), M (58), VC (34), VN (11)	110
T	LEYTON	T (77)	77
TB	BROMLEY	MA (9), MRL (14), T (67)	90
TC	CROYDON	L (40), M (55)	95
TH	THORNTON HEATH	DT (11), L (69), T (11)	91
TL	CATFORD	DW (7), LA (13), MW (14), SR (23), T (78)	135
U	UPTON PARK	RML (26), S (36), T (42)	104
UX	UXBRIDGE	LS (7), LX (5), M (35), MA (36), MT (2)	85
V	STAMFORD BROOK	DT (22), L (21), LX (5), M (36), MRL (4)	88
W	CRICKLEWOOD	DR (9), LN (19), M (47)	75
WK	STANWELL	CV (4), DA (7), LS (11)	22
WN	WOOD GREEN	DRL (13), M (81)	94
X	WESTBOURNE PARK	DW (74), M (27), RML (41)	142
TOTAL SCHEDULED			4034

LS allocations at NS and PM are Mobility Buses. Allocations do not include vehicles permanently positioned for contract or private hire purposes. Garages with Routemasters only use these on Mondays to Saturdays and are all-opo on Sundays. Other garages are all-opo daily. RA is closed at weekends; S, NW and WK are closed on Sundays. Correct to 24th April 1993.